Financial
Modelling
for Business
Decisions

THE CHARTERED
INSTITUTE OF
MANAGEMENT
ACCOUNTANTS
CIMA

Financial Modelling for Business Decisions

BRYAN
KEFFORD

KOGAN
PAGE

First published in 1995

Apart from any fair dealing for the purposes of research or private study, or criticism or review, as permitted under the Copyright, Designs and Patents Act, 1988, this publication may only be reproduced, stored or transmitted, in any form or by any means, with the prior permission in writing of the publishers, or in the case of reprographic reproduction in accordance with the terms of licences issued by the Copyright Licensing Agency. Enquiries concerning reproduction outside those terms should be sent to the publishers at the undermentioned address:

Kogan Page Limited
120 Pentonville Road
London N1 9JN

© Bryan Kefford, 1995

British Library Cataloguing in Publication Data

A CIP record for this book is available from the British Library.

ISBN 0 7494 1635 1

Typeset by Kogan Page
Printed and bound in Great Britain

Contents

profiles; Calculations using cost profiles; Switching
and selection; Model structure; Tuning the model;
Summary.

List of Figures

1

Introduction

Late one Friday, many years ago, I was desperately trying to complete a profit forecast for the Board. As ever in these situations, a very critical piece of information was missing, namely the cost of sales for the last quarter of the year. I had little choice but to make the assumption that this would be the same ratio to sales as the previous three quarters. Alas, the product mix turned out to be very different. The storm that broke over me a month later made me realise there were two things I had to come to terms with. First, there is no necessary correlation between what had happened before and what might happen in the future. Second, the detailed and integrated calculations required to forecast the business more accurately could not be done by manual methods in the time available. Invention though, as is so often the case, was born out of necessity and ever since I've been striving to devise better ways of helping a business produce its forecasts and make its financial decisions.

BUSINESS DECISIONS

I suppose it's merely stating the obvious, but business decisions, or indeed any decisions, can only affect future events. To make informed decisions therefore, we need to know as much as possible about the ways in which the business might be affected by them in the future. Figure 1.1 shows the way in which most decisions affect the business financially. There is usually some form of investment involved and the decision has to be taken whether or not to proceed with that investment. Perhaps a big cash outlay is needed to provide new production facilities or set in motion a new project development, or it may simply be cash to be paid out before we can get it back in sales. The level and timing of the cash returns that this investment generates will determine whether or not it is worth going for. How we forecast these future events will therefore influence our decision to proceed.

Most business operations are quite complex and the future financial effects of decisions taken now are not at all easy to determine. Not only does the business operation or project have to be clearly understood, but so does the financial model, or the way in which the various financial transactions relate to each other. The whole process of financial forecasting also has to take place as quickly as possible if the results are to be of any use. If manual methods are employed it is almost impossible to get other than a single view of the business case in the time available. Alternatives and options, though, clearly need to be explored at the same time so that decisions can be based on a wider range of possible scenarios.

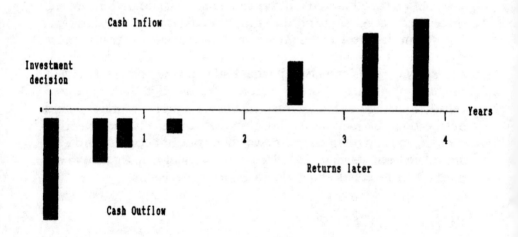

Figure 1.1   Business Decisions

THE COMPUTER FACTOR

My solution to these problems has always been to use computers, but despite vast improvements in technology over the years and extensive use of computers in other fields, the world of financial forecasting has tended to resist such changes until recently. Apart from some strategic planning modelling, there were few people trying to do the same thing as I was. Even now there are not many in the finance and business areas who are prepared to depart from traditional ways of producing forecasts, or even of evaluating new projects. Finance directors, normally charged with producing financial forecasts for the business, have always been, with some notable exceptions, very suspicious of the computer solution.

The use of computer modelling, or simulation, which I have tried to develop for financial forecasting, has been employed extensively in engineering applications. Production has been automated, aero engines have been designed and developed, aircraft have been flown and pilots have been trained, all by computer simulation – and that's only in the aero business. All these applications use the computer's power to calculate. However, most financial and accounting applications simply use computers to keep the records and accounts of the business and to print out information in a presentable form. Where calculations are done, they are managed by different departments, or individuals, and are rarely integrated into a simulation of the whole business or project. The accountant's main role has been of stewardship of the business when the biggest contribution he could make to the decisions that run the business is in financial forecasting. Probably the reason for this emphasis on stewardship is the way historical profits form the basis of financial performance. Cash forecasting, a far more reliable pointer to the success or failure of the business, rarely gets the same level of resources or attention.

The power of computers has increased so much over the years that the desktop machine has now usurped the position of the mainframe computer. During this transition, the way a computer is used has also changed – from centralised computing to distributed computing – where everyone tends to do their own thing. The mainframe computer I started using over 20 years ago, to try to forecast cash receipts, was a thermionic monster built to do engineering calculations. I only managed to get a tiny workspace, just enough for about a dozen lines of program in a very low-level language. A small programmable calculator bought today for a few pounds would have much more power than I had then.

The use of mainframe computers was different in several ways from that of PC-based spreadsheets as can be seen in Figure 1.2. If you wanted to input data, you had to name and define the variables or spaces that would hold that data, then build a program that would interface with you to accept and validate data and enter it into the right place in the right variable. To see that data, you had to build another program that would display a table on the monitor, or print it out if you didn't have a monitor. With a spreadsheet you can always see data that has been entered. The construction of a model to use that data was very similar to a spreadsheet model, except that with the mainframe computer you had to have a data map to remind you how data was stored. Again, the model run program had either to display or print out the results. With the spreadsheet you can see the results of calculations, so a printout, although perhaps desirable, is not essential.

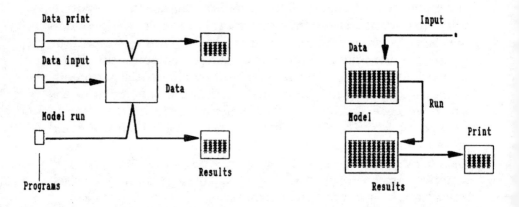

Figure 1.2   Computer-based Financial Models

This advance from low-level computer languages to higher level applications like spreadsheets has certainly improved the user interface. It has also significantly speeded up the process of building financial models. However, the way in which models can be built to produce financial forecasts has changed very little. In terms of calculations, no more can be done on a spreadsheet now than when I first got serious on a mainframe. The same goes for more recent software advances such as using a mouse with a windows screen rather than operating entirely through the keyboard. These advances all relate to display and user interfaces. The user still has to build the model and the most powerful language for doing that was the IBM APL language. However, the point is that the principles and practice of building financial models are as valid now as they were 20 years ago, except that I've probably clarified the grey areas a little and devised a few techniques better adapted to PC spreadsheets.

With spreadsheets, or any other software packages, I find that I use only those functions or parts of the program that I need; meaning that only a part of any program is of use to me. Having said this, when designing a modelling application it helps if the facilities available in a program are well understood. Once there is familiarity with a package and it does what is needed, then it pays to stick with it. Learning to use another can be very time-consuming and can also make the previous work redundant. For these reasons and also for the reason that most spreadsheets these days have mostly the same functions and facilities, I have not been too specific about the use of particular programs or functions in this book. I have always used versions of the SuperCalc spreadsheet, by Computer Associates International, Inc., running on the Microsoft MS-DOS operating system. Users of other spreadsheets and operating systems will have little difficulty in adapting any of the commands or functions that I have used.

Please do not assume that the way I do something is the only way. There is always more than one way of doing anything in financial modelling. All I can hope for this book is that it gives the reader ideas and a working framework within which they might start to build financial models, or devise ways of improving their present techniques. The message is that computer-based modelling techniques are far better for producing financial forecasts and appraisals than manual, or other unintegrated calculation methods.

THE FINANCIAL FORECASTING SCENE

Figure 1.3 shows how a modelling approach can change the way in which financial forecasts are usually prepared. The diagram at the top represents the normal method, which depends on the involvement of different functions within the business to produce their own part of the final forecast. The financial function is shown as coordinating the process and collecting the various inputs together, before producing the overall financial presentation. The production area has to wait for a sales demand level from marketing before it can derive the load on its workshops. It can then calculate the resources it would need to do the job, as well as establishing the resulting stock levels. Part of this production load might also come from engineering's requirements as part of developing new products or prototypes.

Looking at the top diagram in Figure 1.3, you will see that after the forecast has been produced, it would be reviewed by the managing director and, no doubt, be found wanting in some way. That particular view of the future may not be too palatable and the business might need to see how it could change the way investment or programme assumptions had been made. Part of the forecast would therefore need to be referred back to production and, perhaps, to engineering for them to recalculate using the changed assumptions. If the forecast looked particularly bleak, the whole forecast may be repeated using quite different assumptions about how the business could go forward.

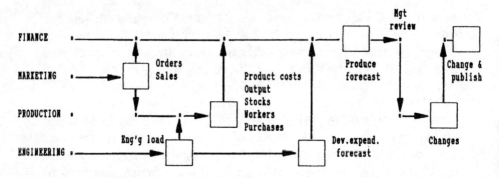

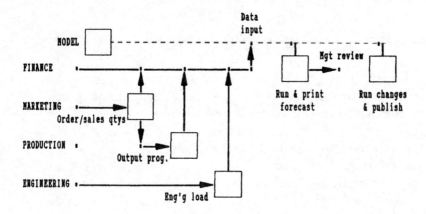

Figure 1.3 Financial Forecasting Methods

There are distinct disadvantages in this way of producing forecasts:

- ☐ A lot of people are involved
- ☐ The process takes a long time
- ☐ It is difficult to make changes or to see 'what happens if?'
- ☐ Different people and departments will have varying levels of optimism and accuracy
- ☐ Central reviews are difficult because knowledge and detail stays in the areas producing each part of the forecast
- ☐ It is difficult to handle progressive calculations such as Sales to Load/Capacity to People Costs to Product Costs if these calculations are done in different areas
- ☐ You can never be sure that the whole forecast is based on common assumptions and levels of business, even though these may have been agreed to start with.

THE MODELLING APPROACH

All such disadvantages can be overcome if the calculations are integrated into a single model. The lower part of Figure 1.3 shows what effect this can have. The marketing, production and engineering functions still have an involvement, but their inputs are of data at a much lower level. They do very little calculation, but still have the responsibility for the information that only they can provide; for example, programme quantities and loads instead of sales values and production expenditure.

The overall preparation time is reduced dramatically and a complete forecast can be printed out almost as soon as the last data have been checked and entered into the model. Even more dramatic is the reduction in time required to change the forecast and publish revised results. Different scenarios can also be explored so that ways can be found to devise product or investment strategies to optimise the performance of the business. All this for only the modest investment of time that it takes to build the model.

The integration of calculations in a model ensures that all the results are coming from a common base of low-level data, which is itself forecast by those with the specialist knowledge. Once it has been proved that a model will give expected results, it can be used to produce credible forecasts time after time, with only the smallest changes to the low-level data variables. The accounting principles and report formats can be built into the model and thereafter come out right every time. Arithmetical accuracy is improved, and it also becomes more difficult to miss something out because of the controls built into the model.

It is only possible to model a business properly if there is a full understanding of how it works. The very process of building a model, therefore, gives a better insight into the business operation and aids the process of understanding what makes it tick. Because a model can produce complete results very quickly it can be used, not only to investigate different scenarios, but also to test the effects of specific risks to the business that are associated with a new project or sales bid. The probability of different events occurring can be assessed by running the model many times under different conditions. The factors that make this possible are the short time it takes to run a forecast and the small amount of manual intervention required.

ABOUT THE FOLLOWING CHAPTERS

The content of this book is based on many years of experience. Trying to structure it in a logical way proved to be quite difficult, particularly the sequence of the chapters. Such a sequence defines where you are going to start and finish, so to start at a certain point assumes that the reader's knowledge of the subject also starts there. Business financial modelling is of interest to business managers, project managers and engineers, as well as to accountants and financial planners. Therefore, it is appropriate to start with a financial modeller's view of how to account for the business. This needs to be clearly understood before anything else in financial modelling can be sensibly explained. Although accountants will get a different slant on the subject from Chapter 2, they will not feel it is entirely wasted on them. The modelling approach to business problems makes you look at things in a different way, as you will find out in due course.

Following on from this basic understanding of how funds flow round the business, Chapter 3 is devoted to explaining the process of expenditure distribution and product costing. This is the part of the financial model that covers factory operations, which can be the most complex part of the business to model.

The next two chapters (4 and 5) explore the techniques and

practice of building models of the business, both for long-term and for shorter term forecasts, each demanding different methods. Within these chapters most of the modelling principles will be covered. Then follows a chapter (6) that covers the need that most businesses have for a flexible reporting system. This can be used to present the results from forecasting models, compare them with actuals and budgets and consolidate the various companies within a business group. I again use the same spreadsheet modelling techniques, but in a different way.

The following chapter (7) looks at the way in which new projects and bids for new business can be evaluated. Part of this chapter is devoted to an explanation of how such projects can be valued and compared, by discounting their future cashflows. All too often, people make such appraisals simply on the strength of profits or cost savings, but fail to understand the full implications of cashflow timing and its effect on the value of that project to the business. At the end of this chapter I've shown how models can be used to evaluate the possible effects on the business of risks associated with such projects, but without delving into the mathematics of probability and decision trees.

In the first part of the penultimate chapter (8), there is a guide to how models can be designed and built to come together easily and be operated efficiently. Following this are the dos and don'ts of financial modelling on spreadsheets, which are designed to reduce the risk of errors and omissions. The integrity of a model used to make business judgements is, of course, paramount. Essentially this chapter is a set of notes and guidelines on how to practice good modelling techniques.

Finally Chapter 9 covers worked examples of forecasting for business decisions, based on a small bicycle manufacturing business. Although the facts and figures of the business are hypothetical, I did have experience of such a company in the past and have attempted to make its operations as realistic as possible. The small size of the business makes it possible to show the picture more clearly, but the nature of the engineering and decision processes involved are as complex as a much larger business. The modelling and decision analysis techniques that are used can therefore be read across to almost any manufacturing or to any other kind of business. The only real differences will be the number of products and scale of operation.

TOOLS OF THE TRADE

When I started building financial models, I felt concerned at not using queuing theory or linear programming, when perhaps I should. However, all I've ever needed are basic arithmetic and algebra, plus the help of some of the powerful little functions that come with a spreadsheet. As far as algebra is concerned, it is mainly a question of being able to construct a formula to make the calculation you want and understanding the order of precedence of each operator in the spreadsheet.

I think a model should be kept as simple as possible, as long as that is consistent with modelling the business as closely as possible. Simplicity engenders clarity of thought. There is nothing so disturbing as trying to find out why a complex formula is giving a ridiculous answer and then having to change the logic completely in order to make sense of it. You can sometimes end up having to restructure large parts of the spreadsheet. There are times when the formula necessarily becomes complex, but it always pays to avoid complication wherever possible. Having said this, if you are one of the elite band of modellers who can find a use for the calculus or other mathematical pursuits and can still remember how to do them, then I'm sure you will go far. The rest of us mere mortals, though, will keep it simple so that we can see what we are doing.

The only other skills I think you will need, to make use of this book, are a basic working knowledge of how to use a computer and spreadsheet software, together with a logical, questioning approach to business problems. I wish you well.

2

The Financial Model

The main objective of any business is to profit from the cash invested in it. Accounting for the way the business achieves this objective is done by means of a set of books, which record all the financial transactions that take place. The flow of funds through the business is monitored in this way so that, at any time, we know how the cash has been invested and what return or profit has been made so far.

Businesses can be very different in the way that cash flows round them, but they all have a common basis of accounting for performance: the books. To be able to forecast the financial performance of a business we have to start from these books and predict the way they will change with time. So we have to understand the basic financial model, represented by the set of books, as well as the way a specific business will relate to that model, before we can produce a complete business forecasting model.

In this chapter I am going to explain the financial set of books from the point of view of someone wanting to build a model of the business. There is no hiding place for such a person. If there is not a proper understanding of how funds flow round the business, there can be no model that will reliably forecast future performance. These explanations of the financial model will unavoidably be lessons in accounting, but I am sure that even those well versed in such disciplines will find it useful to look at things in this way. It is certainly essential reading for understanding the structures of models and modelling techniques that I will cover in later chapters.

The use of diagrams is an essential part of these explanations and makes it possible to see more clearly how relationships and other modelling assumptions can be created. It will be a technique that I will use throughout this book to explain not only concepts and ideas, but also the structures of spreadsheet models that lend themselves naturally to this method of presentation.

INVESTMENT IN THE BUSINESS

Figure 2.1 shows an overview of a business financial model. The lines represent the flow of funds round the business and the arrows the direction of flow. These lines, in book-keeping terms, are transactions that move funds from one account to another. The accounts are shown as boxes in this diagram and they all have a timing difference of some sort between transactions coming in and transactions going out. In other words, they each have a balance or value at a given point in time, which could be either positive or negative. Because what comes out of one account goes into another, the sum of these account balances is zero, the balance sheet of the business. This equal and opposite effect of every transaction gives rise, of course, to the term double-entry bookkeeping.

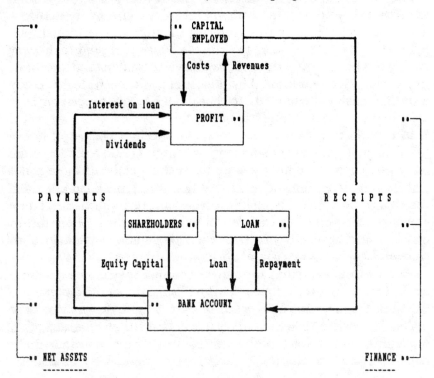

Figure 2.1   Investment in the Business

Before a business can start operating it needs some form of cash injection. It needs initial cash to acquire premises and make the first products, due to the time it will take to get enough back from customers to finance this. The initial investment in the business normally comes from the owners, sometimes a single owner in a small business, sometimes shareholders who share ownership. This equity capital is shown coming out of the shareholders' account and into the bank account. The bank balance at that time would become positive, a business asset, and the shareholders' account balance would be negative, which means it represents the liability of the business to the shareholders for the cash they have put in. At some point in time, when the business has made some profit, the shareholders would expect to get a dividend or return on their investment and this is shown as a payment of cash and a charge against profits.

If the owner or shareholders cannot provide sufficient finance, or if there is a short-term need for extra funds, then cash could also be borrowed from a bank or other finance house and, again, this loan would be cash flowing out of the loan account and into the bank account. The loan agreement would define the way in which repayment with interest would be made. Interest paid would be charged against profit and the repayment of capital borrowed would go to reduce the loan balance. The balance on the loan account would be negative and represent, at any point in time, the liability of the business for the outstanding balance.

The business uses the cash stake to buy property and plant and to make and sell goods. The size of this capital employed in the business will depend largely on the time taken between making payments and receiving cash back into the bank. It is this net cashflow that will decide how the business can expand or even whether it can survive. Therefore, the less that is locked up in capital employed, the better the cashflow and the better the profit or return on the cash invested. Capital employed plus the bank balance comprise the net assets of the business.

Profit account initially represents the amount by which revenues from sales to customers have exceeded the costs of the business to date. If a business is making a profit, then this profit will come back into cash and the business will end up with more in the bank than it started with. Some part of profits is also distributed to shareholders as dividends and paid as interest on loans. The balance that remains is that which has been retained or re-invested in the business and forms a part of the finance of the business, along with share and loan capital accounts.

MAKING A PROFIT

In Figure 2.2 the source of finance from equity or loan capital has been left off and the capital employed has been expanded to show stocks and customer accounts. Capital employed is hardly ever that simple, but for the purposes of this diagram there is an assumption that the business neither owns any property or plant nor buys anything on credit. What I want to show in this section is how a profit is generated and how profit relates to cashflow.

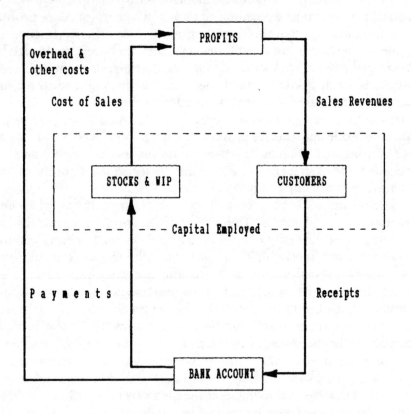

Figure 2.2   Making a Profit

Sales take place at a point in time. There is a specific time for each sale when title, or ownership, in the goods or services changes from the supplier to the customer. At the point of sale the sales value goes through the books as a transaction out of profit account and into the customer's account. The positive balance on the customer's account at that time represents the amount owed to the business. The gross profit on the sale is also recorded at this time by transferring the cost of the sale out of stocks and offsetting it against the sales value in the profit account. This cost of sale, however, only includes the costs that can be attributed to the particular product or service that is sold. Out of the resultant gross profit must come the indirect or overhead costs of the business plus other costs such as interest on loans, royalties for manufacturing under licence, costs of developing new products and, ultimately, the distribution of profit as dividends.

Before sales can be made and the cost of sales transferred out of stocks, the goods to be sold must be purchased or manufactured and the services to be sold have to be provided. This all involves the business in spending its cash, usually over a period of time, which for a large project could be a number of years. The ongoing expenditure and intermittent sales will mean that there will be a positive balance of stocks, which will include, in a manufacturing business, part-completed units or work-in-progress (WIP).

There is clearly a relationship between profits and cashflow. All profit ultimately becomes the net cashflow, although there may be a big time difference between the two. Sales drive the receipts from customers, so we could model receipts by defining their relationship to sales. Cost of sales, which is also driven by sales, itself drives payments for buying and manufacturing stocks. So we could model these payments by defining the way in which they relate to cost of sales. Sales and cost of sales, though, can be made up of many units of different products sold to many different customers. It may be necessary, therefore, to define relationships with payments and receipts for all the variations of product and customer.

There is another way that the net cashflow (receipts less payments) can be calculated, which can be useful in models that set out to generate longer term or strategic forecasts of the business, where such detail is either not required or not available. Profits can be calculated quite easily, being largely driven by the forecast of sales and reduced by other operating costs and development. We can get to net cashflow by taking this profit and deducting any increase in capital employed (or adding a decrease). So, using the model in Figure 2.2, profit less the sales locked up in customer accounts and less the expenditure paid for, but still locked up in stocks and WIP, gives the net cashflow of the business over the same time period. The relationships of sales to customer balance and cost of sales to stocks, that can be used to derive cashflow in this way, can be made much more generalised and revolve around type of customer or product, rather than all the detailed variations.

These relationships between sales, profits and cashflow are at the core of financial models of the business. It is usually not too difficult to forecast profits if we know what sales are, but invariably much more difficult to calculate what the cashflow or the capital employed would be. Computer-based spreadsheet models therefore give the business the ability to integrate these calculations to forecast cash and capital employed as well as profit and to forecast rapidly how these would change if sales were to change.

EXPENDITURE AND COSTS

Most goods and services that a business buys are bought on credit. It takes possession of them now and pays the supplier later. Because of this timing difference, accounts are created for suppliers that contain the balance due to them. This would normally be a negative balance because the flow of purchases into the business from the supplier is recorded before payment is made in settlement.

Sometimes, when the supplier has to finance manufacture of the goods that have been ordered and there will be a long lead time before delivery, some part of the value may be required as a deposit with order, or progress payments may be required at different stages of manufacture. Such payments are shown in Figure 2.3 as cash flowing from the bank to an account called 'progress payments to suppliers'. The balance on this account represents the amount due back from the supplier if the goods are not delivered. When the supplier delivers and final payment becomes due, the deposit previously paid is deducted by clearance from the progress payment account and the remaining balance is paid out of the bank account. It is important that such terms of payment are properly understood if the cashflow of the business is to be modelled accurately.

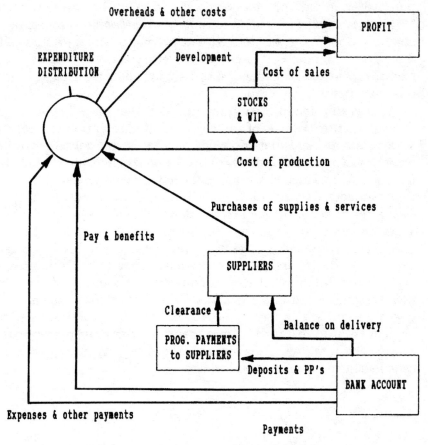

Figure 2.3 Expenditure and Costs

The expenditure of the business that is not paid for on credit is paid directly out of the bank account. The largest part of this, and very often the largest part of total expenditure, is the payroll cost, net pay to employees and PAYE, NI and other deductions paid out. Other payments that are paid straight away will be those such as expenses paid to employees, commissions to agents, royalties to licensees and interest plus charges to the bank.

Figure 2.3 shows that all this expenditure is going into a circle called 'expenditure distribution'. This is because, although suppliers are paid in the same way regardless of the nature of purchases from them and all work by employees is paid for in the same payroll, the business needs to differentiate between the objects of this expenditure to understand what is going on in the business. That part of purchases and pay that goes directly into manufacturing products for sale needs to be identified separately so that capital employed in stocks and WIP can be derived and products can be costed out. Again, development costs and other overheads need to be built up from the sources of expenditure, namely purchases, payroll and other payments.

This distribution of expenditure usually takes place in two ways. For expenditure that can be directly attributed to a product a coding system is employed that identifies purchases and payroll costs to work or job numbers. Indirect or overhead expenditure can only be included in product costs by apportioning it between the work centres involved in manufacture, and then sharing out the costs to each product going through the work centre, usually by calculating a cost rate based on predicted workload.

In terms of modelling cashflow, therefore, product costs, development, overheads and other costs need to be analysed by source of expenditure. All these slices of payroll, expenses and purchases can then be synthesised into payments. When a workload base is used to cost products with a cost rate, the product cost will also need to be defined in terms of the hours spent on each unit in each work centre. The total hours loaded into each work centre can then be established and a cost rate calculated.

BUILDINGS AND PLANT

For a business to operate it normally needs premises, plant and equipment. If these are leased or rented, then the payments for lease or rent will be part of the costs of running the business. As such, they would be treated like other expenditure, ending up within product costs or overheads and being charged against profits. However, if the buildings and plant are owned by the business, there will be no costs to be accounted for in that way. But buildings and plant will not last forever and the business needs to allow for the drop in value, or depreciation, of these assets over the period of their expected lives. This depreciation is calculated as annual increments that will reduce the original values to zero by the time the asset lives expire. It is entered in the books as a transaction that increases expenditure and reduces the balance on the buildings and plant account. Depreciation can be a very significant addition to costs when the business has complex and expensive manufacturing facilities.

In practice the different types of buildings and plant, or fixed assets, of the business are held in separate accounts, which also segregate their original cost (positive balance) from their aggregate depreciation to date (negative balance). This is because depreciation is calculated on the cost of each asset, as is the Inland Revenue capital allowance for depreciation in taxable profit calculations. There is also a need to have control over the large investment in fixed assets and the accounts are normally supported by detailed records of individual purchases and acquisitions, which can have existence and location verified by audit.

Throughout the life of the business there will be additions to these fixed assets, shown in Figure 2.4 as capital expenditure purchases. There may also be disposals or sales of assets previously acquired and in this case the transaction would set the aggregate depreciation against the original cost and transfer the resultant net book value to profit account. When the selling value of the assets is entered against the book value in profit account the profit or loss on sale will be recorded there.

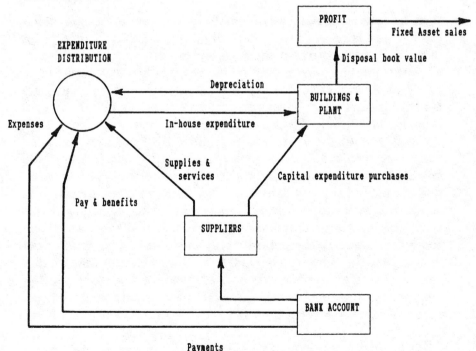

Figure 2.4 Buildings and Plant

Capital expenditure is not always purchased. Sometimes buildings, plant and equipment, or parts of them, are created in-house within the business itself. Usually it is only the internal labour cost that is involved, but a business making motor vehicles, for example, could well capitalise complete vehicles for its own use in this way. The in-house labour would be costed through the process of expenditure distribution mentioned before, so that both the pay and a share of the overheads is attributed to the cost.

Depreciation, although treated by the business as a cost and charged against profits, is not a cash payment. The cash payment involved is the purchase of the buildings or plant in the first place. So, in our model, we can convert the profit effect (depreciation) into cashflow (fixed asset purchase payment) by deducting the increase, or adding a decrease, in the buildings and plant account, in the same way as stock and customer accounts were treated.

SALES REVENUES AND VAT

With large or long lead time orders there are often terms agreed that call for the customer to pay a deposit up front with the order, or for progress payments to be made at various milestones in the contract. Even the amount outstanding on delivery to the customer may be partly retained and paid some time later, perhaps when the main contractor finally commissions the plant. Receipts under the contract due before delivery to the customer would be accounted for as a cashflow into the bank account and out of an account called 'customer deposits and prog. payments'. The transaction would create a negative balance on this account representing the amount due to the customer if the business failed to complete the contract. As we saw with supplier progress payments, when the delivery was made the bill to the customer would be netted down on the customer's account by the deposits previously paid. The amount deducted from the bill would be transferred from the customer account to the customer deposit account, so clearing that balance. The customer would then pay the net amount outstanding on the customer account, part of it later if a retention had been called for in the contract.

If a business is registered for VAT we can see from Figure 2.5 that it has to collect the tax from its customers and pay it out to its suppliers. The incidence of the tax will depend on the extent to which supplies are exempt or zero rated. In the final analysis the net of the amounts collected and paid out will be settled by payment to (or receipts from) Customs and Excise. For a registered business there is therefore no effect on profits nor, in the end, on cashflow. But the timing of the various transactions involved can significantly influence the short-term cashflow of the business.

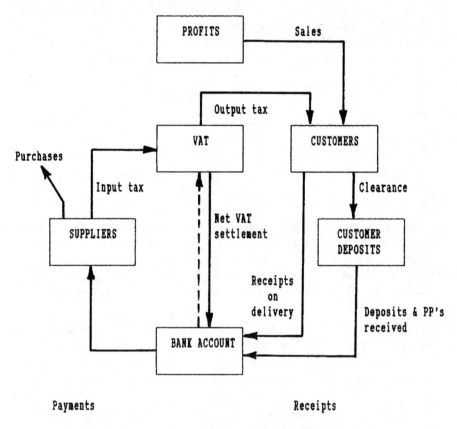

Figure 2.5 Sales Revenues and VAT

It is tempting, in building a business model, to ignore VAT. If the forecast required is long-term then VAT can be ignored, but if short-term cash forecasts are required then it almost certainly pays to include it. Leaving it out of a business model also leaves open the possibility of the model becoming inaccurate or incomplete if things change in the future. For example, tax rates could change making for larger amounts of cash involved, or the business could make changes in the volume of export sales. If VAT had been modelled there would be no problem in assessing the effect of such changes on cashflow. If it had not been modelled then the business might well feel the need to make such calculations to find out the effects and that could be time-consuming. At worst the business might choose to ignore the problem and not foresee a short-term cash need. In business modelling it is prudent not to take short cuts, but attempt to model what is likely to happen as closely as possible. Then if conditions do change you have a reasonable chance of getting a valid forecast of business performance.

FUTURE LOSSES

Profit is king in most business organisations. It is the general measure of success; it is the base for assessing liability to tax; it determines how much investors get in dividends; and it helps to persuade investors to put in more money. Getting a true and fair view of profit locks up most of the resources of the finance department at accounting year-ends. Profit is the difference between revenues we expect to get from sales deliveries in the period and the cost of those sales together with other operating and development costs in the accounting period. The extent to which there is any doubt about the assets created in the trading period, by making sales or building stocks, needs to be allowed for by adjusting profit declared.

If the business does not expect the customer to pay up for the sales that have been delivered and charged to the customer's account, then some reduction would need to be made to the customer debt. In Figure 2.6 a transaction has been shown that makes provision for that possible loss of sales value by creating a 'bad debt provision account' and charging profit account with the expected loss in value. If at some future time it was found that the debt could never be recovered, perhaps because of the customer's business failure, then the amount lost would be written off the customer's account balance and set against the bad debt provision account. In this way, the capital employed would also truly reflect the cash owed to the business, since the customer account would be offset by the negative bad debt provision until such time as any actual bad debts were taken out of the customer account balance.

In the same way that debts could be overstated, the business also has to be sure that what it holds as stock is also saleable. This usually means trying to equate the stockholding with a forecast of future sales by product. In a manufacturing business, with quite a long manufacturing cycle, work might have been started or completed before any orders had been received, or any firm prospects had been identified. The bottom might have fallen out of the market forecast since production programmes had last been considered and some of the current stock and WIP might be considered surplus to requirements. Such a surplus could also build up on any stockholding because the product had become redundant or out-of-date. The business would account for surplus stocks by creating a 'stock provision' account and charging profit account with the expected loss in value of the stocks, in exactly the same way that debts were written down. If and when the business scrapped or disposed of that surplus, then its stock value would be written out of the stock account and offset against the stock provision.

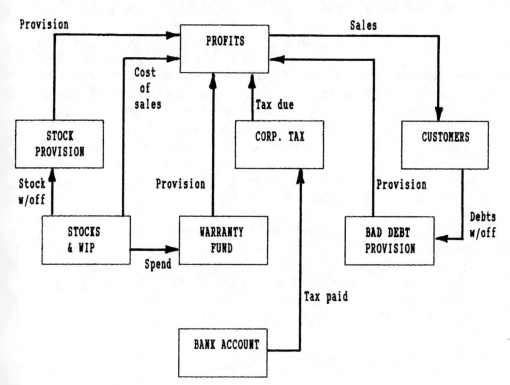

Figure 2.6 Future Losses and Profits Tax

When a business makes sales to its customers it also usually gives them some warranty or guarantee that its products will meet the customer's needs and not fail within a certain time. If failures do occur the business undertakes to repair or replace the faulty product, usually at no cost to the customer. Over a period of time, of course, there will be failures and resultant rectification costs incurred by the business. The longer the view that the business has of such occurrences the better idea it will have of the average cost per unit sold that it should provide for warranty.

Therefore, when the business makes sales, it needs to take account of these future costs of warranty. It does so by creating a warranty fund account and charging profit account with the estimated future costs of warranty relating to the sales made in the period. As and when repair or replacement costs are incurred against warranties, the work done or stocks used to meet these demands are taken out of the stock and WIP account and charged against the warranty fund.

At the end of the accounting year the warranty fund would need to be reviewed. The balance held against each product would be compared with the level of sales made that were still within the warranty period. In that way, the fund could be kept at a level that reflected the future cost liability, by releasing any surplus or charging any additional requirement to profit account.

Another future payment that has to come out of profits is the assessment of tax due, which in the case of companies is Corporation Tax. In order to forecast its profits for distribution to shareholders the company needs to calculate the tax due and set up a corporation tax account to reflect this liability, charging profit account with the value. Corporation Tax is paid in two stages, first as Advance Corporation Tax (ACT) which is paid quarterly on its dividends, then later as the balance of the assessment after deducting ACT paid. These payments are made out of bank account and reduce the tax liability in the corporation tax account.

THE DYNAMIC MODEL

The complete financial model, shown in Figure 2.7, is a representation of the books of a business and the way in which cash flows round it. You will see that an addition has been made to the

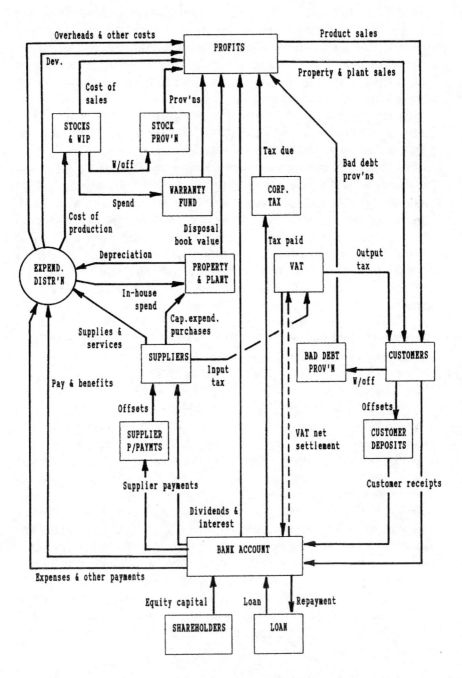

Figure 2.7   The Financial Model

transactions discussed previously to show the payment of dividends and interest out of profits. There may be variations or further transactions and accounts in particular firms, but this model essentially represents the financial affairs of any business. However, it only gives a static view. There are factors that have to be added to turn it into a dynamic model.

The first is the time dimension. The inputs and outputs of the accounts will occur at different times relative to each other and at different rates of flow. Some transaction flows will occur at specific times, some intermittently and some continuously. Sales, for example, will be determined by the forecast program of deliveries for each product, based on orders taken and expected. However, the receipts from those sales will depend on the terms of payment around those deliveries, both before and after. The supply of parts into WIP and stocks might have a relationship to sales. Alternatively, it could have a more direct relationship to a production program designed to even out the workload. The flow of parts might follow a cost profile that gradually rises over the early part of the production cycle. Payment for those parts, however, will depend not only on this incidence of purchases, but also on the terms of payment with the supplier.

Another factor involved is the size of all the transaction values. They will, in many cases, be inter-related. Receipts from customers, for example, can usually be related to sales by percentage of price. Again, payment for expenditure will be related to the proportions of cost that come from each source. Some values such as development of new products, on the other hand, could depend solely on management decisions or on the need to optimise investment returns.

It is all these variables and relationships that turn the static financial model we have been exploring into a dynamic business model. In the following chapters of this book I will show how this can be done. The basic principles we have been looking at in this chapter will provide a good platform for understanding the techniques involved. First though, the next chapter expands on the concept of expenditure distribution, shows how this can be modelled, and looks in more detail at the way in which product costs can be forecast.

SUMMARY

☐ A business can only be modelled properly if there is firstly an understanding of the way in which the books monitor the funds flowing round it.

☐ Investment in a business is provided by equity capital, loan capital and undistributed profits. This investment equates to the capital employed and bank balance of the business.

☐ The difference between profit and cashflow is the timing of transactions. At the end of a business or project the profit will equal cashflow. Cashflow can be calculated either from earlier or later transactions, or from changes in account balances.

☐ Expenditure is distributed into costs, which can then be used to measure performance. The expenditure sources of costs can be used to calculate cash payments.

☐ Fixed assets are usually created in a business with an initial large cash payment which is then charged against profits over their working lives.

☐ VAT transactions should always be modelled properly in short-term forecasts, in case conditions change and the cashflow effects are overlooked.

☐ Getting the true and fair view required of profit for the period means adjusting for any possible overstatement of assets created or understatement of future liabilities.

☐ The static financial model can be turned into a dynamic business model by applying the dimensions of value and timing which relate to that particular business or project.

3

Business Expenditure and Costs

In Chapter 2, expenditure distribution was explained in principle. This chapter looks at how the expenditure of a business can be turned into product costs with the help of spreadsheet models. Costs are normally the area within the profit equation over which the business has some control. Prices are usually set by market forces and the size of the cost will therefore determine the contribution to profit and, perhaps, the selection of an optimum product mix. The way expenditure is allocated and shared out to product costs is therefore crucial to the way product decisions can be made.

THE COSTING PROCESS

First, I will take an overview of what is to be done to arrive at costs. Figure 3.1 shows a slightly expanded version of the diagram used in Chapter 2 (Figure 2.3). This shows how expenditure becomes costs. Some expenditure, such as parts and capital purchases, can be directly attributed to costs of products or fixed assets, such as buildings, because it is carried out with those objectives and analysed by coding. Other expenditure though, such as pay and expenses, can usually only be allocated to products by sharing the cost of running a workshop among all the products going through it, or in other words, by using a cost rate that is derived from the predicted workload in that workshop.

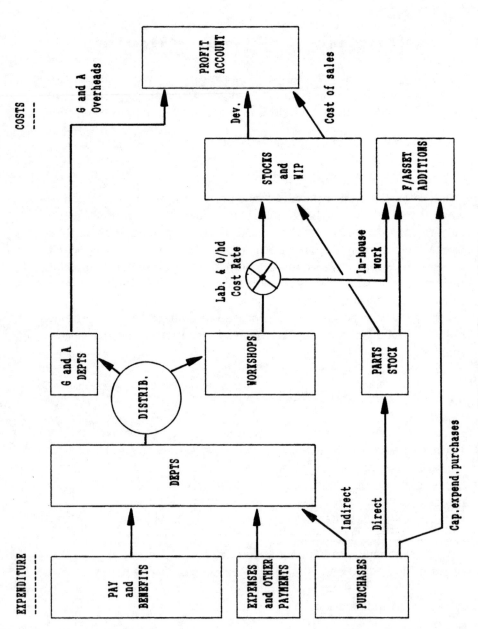

Figure 3.1 Expenditure and Costs

Because cost rates will vary with load, product costs will rise in times of shortage of work, unless drastic measures can be taken to cut back on expenditure, or reduce the number of workshops being used. It is essential therefore, particularly in short-term forecasting models, that the expenditure distribution module can be integrated into the general model so that, when sales programmes change, costs will change accordingly. As most purchases are made directly to satisfy a predicted programme of sales, when the workshop load drops, costs can usually be held down only by reducing the number of people. This is because they are by far the biggest component of other expenditure.

The normal procedure for aggregating the cost of each workshop, process area, or manufacturing cell through which work passes, is first to allocate expenditure to departments and then to distribute the cost of those departments to the work centres according to the way services are given. The distribution model therefore must be capable of building up the pay and expenses against each department or cost centre of the business. It must then define the bases by which the departments give their services, first to each other and ultimately to the cost rate, or final cost centres. The following sections show that there are really only two basic methods of distribution, either in stages or simultaneously. In the real world though, there are probably as many variations on this theme as there are different businesses.

In Figure 3.1, I have shown cost distributed to General and Administrative Departments and being charged against profits account. This treatment reflects the nature of these costs, which are not usually volume or product related and tend to remain much more constant with volume change. Many businesses might equally well include such costs with the distribution to workshops, or there could be just a single cost rate for the whole factory. Some companies also recognise the cost of handling and storing parts by distributing the expenditure on such services to a separate materials rate area and recovering the cost, probably as a percentage, on the materials or parts cost of the product rather than on labour hours. Individual businesses have different needs, and costing methods are in any case some sort of a compromise. There cannot be such a thing as the correct cost of a product, not unless it is the only product from a factory over the period of its manufacturing cycle, and even then, certainty cannot be guaranteed.

DEPARTMENTAL EXPENDITURE

The first stage of our expenditure distribution model therefore must be able to forecast the total pay and expenses that can be attributed to each department or cost centre of the business. In Figure 3.2, and in the following diagrams, I have shown many departments grouped under headings, such as Production Support or Services. This is for simplicity of the diagrams. In practice, all the departments that were separately managed and that were accountable cost centres would be separately analysed and budgeted for in this first stage, though they may well be grouped later for purposes of distribution.

Figure 3.2 shows how the forecast of departmental cost is built up. We are looking at a forecast for a specific period of time, depending on whether the general model is built to handle annual, quarterly, or monthly periods. The link to the general model is via the hours loading calculated from the production output programmes. These hours are first used to calculate the number of direct workers required, which is done by dividing by the utilisation factors applying to each area. These factors will be derived from the proportion of a worker's attendance time that is expected to be effective working time.

The number of indirect workers required will usually be calculated by reference to a known, or expected, ratio of indirect to direct workers within the business department. Planned improvements can be built in to the ratio by changing this variable over a period of time. The number of staff required in a department will usually be an estimate based on past experience and, again adjusted for planned changes.

Once the number of workers has been forecast, the expenditure on pay plus the company contributions to pensions and NI can be calculated from the average pay rates for each class of worker. If shorter term forecasts such as budgets are being produced, the level of detail in these calculations might be increased, for example, to handle differing pay claim dates or different union groupings. Pay inflation coefficients will be applied that reflect the forecast pay strategy of the business.

Expenses that form the remainder of the total departmental expenditures, can be forecast by using an historical relationship to pay and benefits, and by modifying this to reflect any savings and changes that can be predicted. Such savings are best built in to the model as separate variables so that the effect of future changes can be easily investigated.

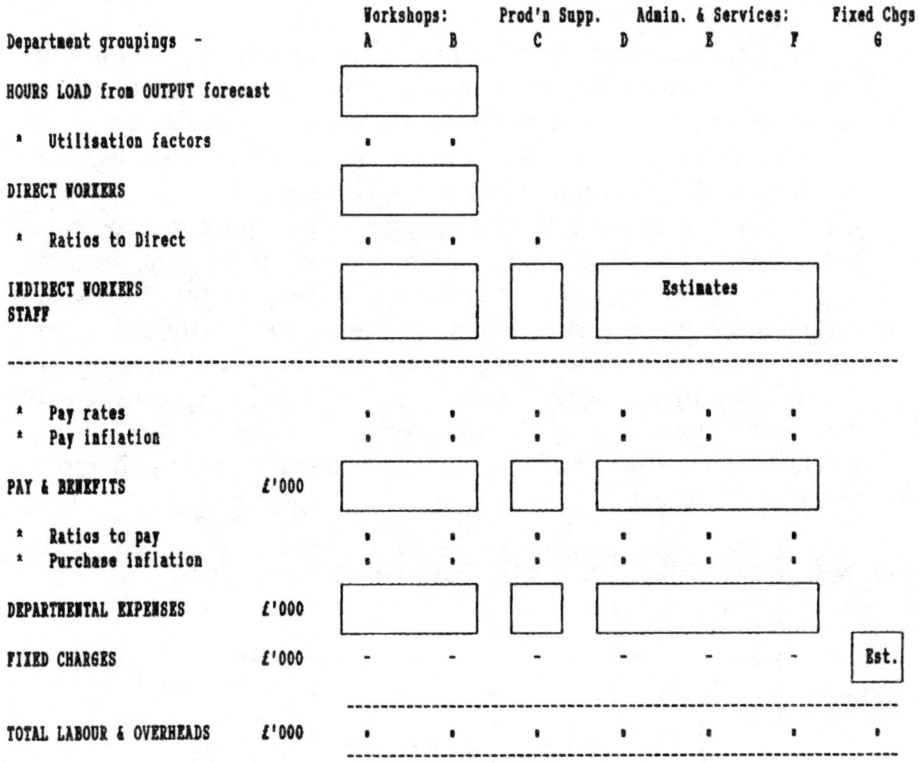

Department groupings -	Workshops: A	B	Prod'n Supp. C	Admin. & Services: D	E	F	Fixed Chgs G
HOURS LOAD from OUTPUT forecast							
* Utilisation factors	•	•					
DIRECT WORKERS							
* Ratios to Direct	•	•	•				
INDIRECT WORKERS STAFF				Estimates			
* Pay rates	•	•	•	•	•	•	
* Pay inflation	•	•	•	•	•	•	
PAY & BENEFITS £'000							
* Ratios to pay	•	•	•	•	•	•	
* Purchase inflation	•	•	•	•	•	•	
DEPARTMENTAL EXPENSES £'000							
FIXED CHARGES £'000	-	-	-	-	-	-	Est.
TOTAL LABOUR & OVERHEADS £'000	•	•	•	•	•	•	•

Figure 3.2 Departmental Expenditure Forecast

To complete the picture of expenditure, an estimate will be made of what I have called fixed charges. These are not necessarily all fixed, some may be semivariable with volume, but they are the sort of costs that cannot be allocated to departments, but have to be distributed to those departments on some basis, such as floor area. They will include costs such as utilities and rates, which the business pays for in total.

DISTRIBUTION BASES

As stated earlier, the departmental expenditure forecast has to be distributed to the final cost rate centres by defining the way services are given to these areas. A set of bases is determined, one for each department or group of departments, and the expenditure previously allocated to each department is shared out in proportion to its base.

There are not many types of base. The three most common are shown in Figure 3.3: floor area, number of people and the manager's estimate (usually as a percentage). Floor area is used as a base for expenditure that is related to space usage, such as rates, lighting, heating and depreciation of buildings. Numbers of people are used where expenditure is related to people. This would include costs such as personnel departments, training, canteen, surgery, fire service and security. Sometimes there are subsets of the number of people base, where costs are identified separately to different categories, such as staff training, or works' canteen. The basis for distributing many departmental services will be an estimate of proportions provided by the manager of the department, who is usually the one who knows best what the department is going to be doing in the future.

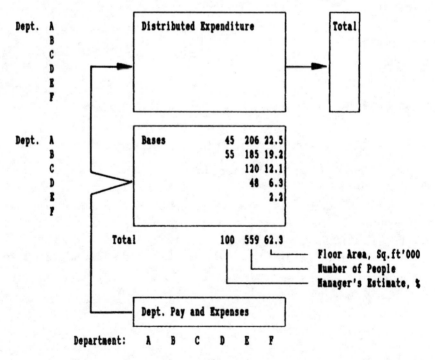

Figure 3.3   Distribution Bases

There are of course other types of base, many no doubt being specific to a particular business. The general principle to be applied is to use a base that is related to the incidence of cost and that can be reasonably forecast. Clearly, the construction of the bases determines the way expenditure is shared out to the cost rate areas. Any doubtful relationship between a base and its cost can affect a cost rate and even the manager's view of the viability of a workshop or manufacturing cell.

In Figure 3.3 you will see that the pay and expenses of each department are apportioned across other departments and the resultant distributed expenditure is finally cross-totalled for each department that has received a share. The object of the exercise is to end up with all the expenditure allocated to the cost rate areas. These departments therefore cannot give their services to others, otherwise, with this single-calculation pass, we will be left with bits of expenditure still in service departments.

The other element to understand about expenditure distribution is where it has come from. The manager of a workshop needs to understand how the cost rate is constructed if action is to be taken to reduce it. So the calculations that are done to distribute expenditure have to show the source as well as the totals distributed. This is most easily done with a staged distribution where no department can give a service to one that has already been distributed. However, this type of distribution, although being simpler, makes it necessary to distort how even cost rate areas give services to other departments. The way to account for all service allocations is to use a simultaneous distribution, but this gives extra problems in seeing where costs are coming from. In the next two sections of this chapter we will look at the two methods, staged and simultaneous distributions, in more detail.

STAGED DISTRIBUTION

If the next two diagrams look rather formidable, don't despair. The arithmetic is quite simple. The first type of distribution I have demonstrated is one that is carried out in stages, shown in Figure 3.4. You will see that the bases are staged so that fixed charges are first distributed to all other departments except themselves, then service departments are distributed progressively (to the left) to all departments except to themselves and those already distributed.

Commercial and Administration (C&A) departments are allowed to give some part of their services to the workshops, but the workshops themselves cannot give any.

The cost that is distributed by each department is its pay and expenses plus any services that have been charged in from departments to the right of it. Taking *Service Dept. E* as an example, the figures in the boxes with solid lines, 400, 23, 14, 0 and 6, are brought down to the total line in the column for *Dept. E* (443) and distributed to the departments in the hatched box above, according to the base below. The same figure that is distributed (443) is then taken out of the *Dept. E* cell so that the total across the line shows only what is left in the department. In the case of a service department, such as *Dept. E*, this is zero.

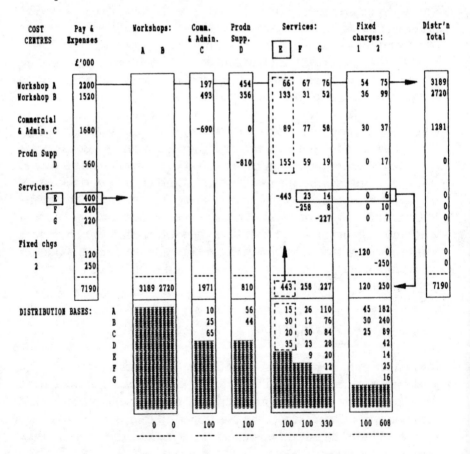

Figure 3.4 Stage Distribution Model

By this means, all the expenditure ends up in the cost rate areas on the top lines, and reading the lines across shows where this expenditure has come from. *Workshop A*, for example, has been attributed with 2200 of its own pay and expenses plus shares of the services from *C&A* (197), *Prodn Support* (454), and so on, all totalling to 3189. The *C&A Dept.* is much the same, except that in its case part of its cost has been distributed to the workshops, the 690 being 35 per cent of all its cost including services given by others.

There are some very definite controls and safeguards needed for this type of model. A spreadsheet cannot handle a division by zero, it will give an error message in the cell. So the formulae that apportion cost into other departments, such as in the cells within the hatched box under *Dept. E*, have an IF statement. This says that if the total of the base is zero, then put in a zero, otherwise calculate the apportioned cost by dividing by the total base and multiplying by the share to the department. Also, the total of the base is a calculated SUM of the elements of that base to ensure that we can see whether or not it does come to 100, or whatever total it should be. Then, as a further check, the total distributed is shown opposite, and on the same line, as the total pay and expenses to be distributed (7190).

Finally, the cells for departments to which we do not want cost distributed are hatched and protected in the base area, so that no bases can be created for them. The only parts of this model that would remain unprotected would be the unhatched base input areas and the pay and expenses input column. If the model was integrated with the general model, which calculated the pay and expenses, even this column would then pull in the figures by formula and also be protected.

SIMULTANEOUS DISTRIBUTION

The model in Figure 3.5 is a logical extension of the staged distribution in Figure 3.4, in which it becomes possible for all departments to give their services to any others simultaneously. There are two restrictions with this method. Service department bases disallow services being given to themselves, thereby ensuring that these departments distribute the whole of their costs. Also, there is no mechanism for departments to charge services to the fixed charge cost centres. This latter constraint is simply to reflect what would not happen in practice, rather than being due to any arithmetic reason.

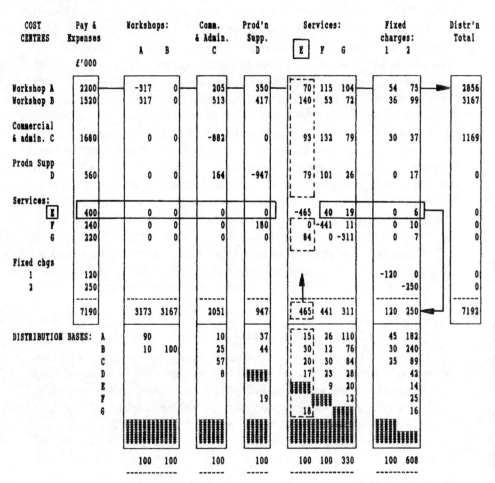

COST CENTRES	Pay & Expenses	Workshops: A	B	Comm. & Admin. C	Prod'n Supp. D	Services: E	F	G	Fixed charges: 1	2	Distr'n Total
	£'000										
Workshop A	2200	-317	0	205	350	70	115	104	54	75	2856
Workshop B	1520	317	0	513	417	140	53	72	36	99	3167
Commercial & admin. C	1680	0	0	-882	0	93	132	79	30	37	1169
Prodn Supp D	560	0	0	164	-947	79	101	26	0	17	0
Services: E	400	0	0	0	0	-465	40	19	0	6	0
F	240	0	0	0	180	0	-441	11	0	10	0
G	220	0	0	0	0	84	0	-311	0	7	0
Fixed chgs 1	120								-120	0	0
2	250									-250	0
	7190	3173	3167	2051	947	465	441	311	120	250	7192
DISTRIBUTION BASES: A		90		10	37	15	26	110	45	182	
B		10	100	25	44	30	12	76	30	240	
C				57		20	30	84	25	89	
D				8		17	23	28		42	
E							9	20		14	
F					19			12		25	
G						18				16	
		100	100	100	100	100	100	330	100	608	

Figure 3.5   Simultaneous Distribution Model

The arithmetic, as you will see, is much the same as for the staged distribution, except that all services received by the department are added to the pay and expenses and distributed upwards, rather than just those to the right. Also, the *workshops* and *C&A* areas work differently. The deduction of 317 in the *Workshop A* cell, for example, not only allows for the total for distribution by the department (3173), as for service areas, but is also offset by the amount retained by *Workshop A*, namely 90 per cent of 3173. This type of formula is also applied to the equivalent cells for *Workshop B* and *C&A*, where they similarly retain part or all of their costs.

Since departments can receive services both before and after a sequential distribution calculation, this spreadsheet model becomes a set of circular calculations. It is actually solving a set of simultaneous equations, hence the name I have given it of simultaneous distribution. The spreadsheet keeps taking out line totals at the right, putting them in at the bottom and redistributing. The computer will keep doing these calculations until the 'delta' or change in the answers has converged to within a specified level of precision or tolerance. I have actually set this spreadsheet to carry out a fixed number of 15 iterations in order to speed up calculation, while at the same time getting the convergence close enough to reduce service departments to zero after rounding.

Comparing the pay and expenses total for distribution with the total distributed shows a difference of 2 (7190 to 7192). This is due to rounding-in the calculations that apply the base percentages, or proportions, to the total department cost. Slightly more accuracy, such as rounding to one or two places of decimals, has been sacrificed to the readability of the page. In a full-size factory distribution with many more cost centres this would be even more appropriate, though the difference itself might well be less significant because of the more evenly balanced gains and losses.

As with the staged distribution model, you will see that the line for each department shows from where it has received all its cost and services, as well as how much it has given to other departments. This line, however, is not the clear source of all its services as was the case with the staged distribution. It is, in fact, a very complex amalgam of percentages of services distributed from percentages of other services. Take the 70 received by *Workshop A* from *Service Dept. E*, for example. It is 15 per cent of the line of cost and services received by *Dept. E*, which is itself made up of figures like the 40, which is 9 per cent of the line for *Dept. F*, and so on.

This type of distribution has the potential for upsetting departmental managers who are trying to understand how their costs come to be so high, but it is a more accurate representation of the incidence of cost based on the way in which the department gives its services. I built my first such model, which we called at that time a reciprocal distribution, on a mainframe computer. Due to the lack of visibility of figures compared to a spreadsheet, I had to do some fancy programming to retain all the slices of the intermediate answers. If the final answers had been given as being the sources of cost then the distribution might have been accepted, but as soon as explanations of the way it worked were attempted, it lost its credibility. Because of this difficulty of understanding where the costs have come from, I suspect that most distribution methods are some form of staged calculations which are simpler to explain.

One more word on staged distributions: the sequence in which the calculation stages take place is crucial to the way services are given. Whatever sequence is used, though, the use of stages compromises in some way the realistic incidence of cost.

WORKLOAD AND CAPACITY

In discussing expenditure and cost rates up to now, I have assumed that demand generated from sales orders can be converted directly into load on the workshops. This can only be a valid assumption if the maximum load is always within the capacity of the business to handle. In other words, the business must have sufficient factory space and equipment, and be able to get the extra people needed with the necessary skills. If these conditions do not apply, the business has several options:

- [ ] Put the work out to sub-contractors, if that is possible
- [ ] Restrict the load to within its capacity either by planning to take less orders, or by being more selective in taking orders, or by spreading the excess load forward into later time periods
- [ ] Invest in a new or larger factory and more equipment
- [ ] Make production more capital intensive, to get more capacity with the same number of people
- [ ] Rent space or other factory premises
- [ ] Buy another business that has the facilities it needs
- [ ] Enter into a joint venture with another business to manufacture the product jointly
- [ ] Acquire extra skilled labour, either by hiring more people or, if the right skills are unavailable outside, by training more people in-house.

All these options, and no doubt others, would be the subject of decisions that the business would have to take nearer the time of the expected peak demand. The way such decisions can be taken more easily by comparing financial evaluations of the possible options are explained in Chapter 7. In any forecasting model though, particularly long-term forecasting, there needs to be a mechanism for comparing load with capacity so that the plan can include assumptions about how excess load will be handled and what effect this will have on product cost.

The forecasting model usually defines workshop capacity in terms of the maximum hours of work that could be handled. The calculated planned workload is then compared with this capacity and any excess is usually assumed to be automatically offloaded to subcontractors. The size of this forecast offload will start the business manager thinking about how this might be handled in the future and whether anything should be done now about new investment. Such expansion can be a very critical time for a business, so the forecasting model needs to give adequate warning of any possible future imbalance of load and capacity.

PRODUCT COSTING

The way a product or contract cost is constructed within a forecast can significantly affect the view taken of the future prospects of the business. In forecasting, we sometimes do not have the benefit of past experience. A product may well be new or a new variant, for which manufacturing times and material content will have to be estimated. At a labour and overheads cost rate of, say 30 per hour, a modest change in expected hours can make a considerable difference to unit cost. If we have had past experience of making the product, averages can be calculated and used for the unit cost of parts and labour hours. Care must be taken here to understand the present time in the life-cycle of the product. Are we still in the learning curve of a young product? Have modifications been made to the design or are any to be made in the future? In other words, the past can never be more than a starting point in such estimates. Care should be taken not to extrapolate actual results without going through the process of trying to find out what is likely to happen in future.

The variables within a product costing equation are the unit value of materials or parts, the unit hours worked in each process or workshop, and the labour and overheads cost rate. We will see in the next chapter how the calculation of loads based on sales demand combines with expenditure distribution to each workshop to give cost rates. The other two variables, materials and labour times, usually have to be estimated by production engineers who will understand the product and how its production methods are likely to change in the future. They will take account of what they know has happened in the past, as well as incorporating predicted cost savings and other changes. As far as our model is concerned, therefore, it is important to allow for the unit cost details to be set up separately in each time period, then such changes in cost profiles can be properly reflected.

SUMMARY

□ Products are costed by being given a share of expenditure attributable to them. Some expenditure can be directly attributed, but some, like pay and overheads, have to be shared out on some equitable basis.

□ Distributing pay and overheads starts with forecasting how much each department will incur and what value there will be of more global fixed costs.

□ These departmental and fixed costs are then distributed to the workshop and administrative overhead cost centres. Cost rates are calculated for workshops in order to cost products going through them and administrative overheads are charged against profit account.

□ There are two basic methods of distributing departmental costs – by staged distribution and by simultaneous distribution.

□ A staged distribution allows for fixed costs and service departments to be distributed in a predetermined sequence. Services cannot be given by workshops or received by departments already distributed. It is easy to see where costs have come from.

□ A simultaneous distribution puts no constraints on how services can be given and more accurately reflects what happens in practice. It is, however, very difficult to demonstrate where costs have come from.

□ A model that calculates cost rates has to make assumptions about how to handle production overcapacity.

□ The costing of new products depends largely on the production engineer's forecast of material content and labour hours required. It also needs to allow for learning curves.

Long-term Forecasting

Having set the financial and costing scenes, we are now going to look at how business forecasts can be produced by building complete models of the business operation. In this chapter I will cover long-term and strategic forecasts and explain some of the basic principles of building forecasts. In the following chapter, the needs of short-term forecasts will be addressed.

It is almost impossible to start to build a model of a business unless the operations of that business and the ways they might change in the future are thoroughly understood. Such operations are best mapped out in the form of an interface chart, which shows how the business interacts with its environment and how work flows round it. Once we have such a chart, then a model can be structured so that it reflects the way the business works.

BUSINESS INTERFACES

If we were to map out the operations of any manufacturing business we would arrive at the sort of chart shown in Figure 4.1. It represents an aero engine repair business that operates from a factory, and has interfaces with its markets for work, its customers, its suppliers, and with inventory that it needs to hold in other parts of the world. It shows the flow of work and parts through the business and identifies the variables that need to be understood if the business is to be modelled. I will explain the operation in more detail because it will help in an understanding of the level of knowledge required to produce such a chart and subsequently model the business. This chart may look complex, but even a small business can look very much the same.

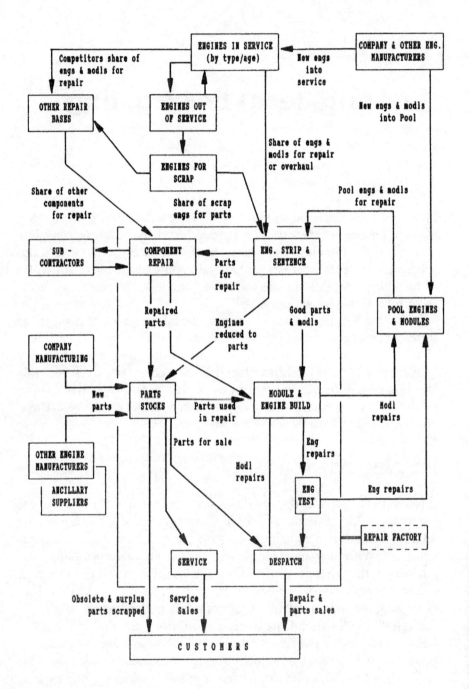

Figure 4.1   Business Interface Chart

The operations carried on in this factory are to repair aero engines that have come in from airlines. Aero engines are built in modular form and modules requiring repair can be removed. Sometimes complete engines come in for repair, sometimes only certain modules. Either way, before anything can be done to the engine or module it has to be inspected and stripped down to see what is wrong. The actual repairs are made to the components or parts, which are sometimes too far gone or too expensive to repair and have to be replaced. Stocks of parts are therefore held, which are used in conjunction with repaired parts, to build the modules and then build the engines back up again. If complete engines are repaired, they are run on test before being despatched to the customer.

Shown on the left of the factory operations are the external sub-contractors who specialise in repairing certain kinds of components and who, perhaps because they do it for other repairers also, can do it more cheaply. The suppliers of parts are also shown. This is mainly the parent company who make most of the engines that are repaired, but also, in a smaller way, other engine manufacturers and makers of ancillary equipment.

Shown on the right of the factory are what are described as pool engines and modules. These represent strategically placed stocks in several parts of the world that are used as temporary replacements for failed units that have to undergo repair. These stand-by units need to be kept in good condition and come in for repair in the same way as engines and modules from customer airlines.

At the bottom of Figure 4.1 are the customers and the supply of parts and services that are provided and sold to them. Sales will be mainly for work done and parts used in repairing engines and modules. Parts will also be supplied to other repair bases where parent company engines are being worked on. These parts could be in replacement for those scrapped, or could be components repaired for the customer. Some repairs can be carried out with the engine still installed. Therefore, the costs of servicing and parts used in these operations will also be sold to the customer airlines. Some parts in stock will ultimately become surplus or obsolete and these will be sold for scrap. The value of such scrap can be quite significant, reflecting the expensive metals used in aero engines.

The top part of Figure 4.1 shows the markets and sources of work coming into the factory. The basic source of engine repair work is the population of engines installed in aircraft that are in service.

Most overhauls and repairs are carried out according to the manu-
facturer's schedule, which sets out the flying hours that should
elapse before certain checks and overhauls have to be made. The
schedule also takes into account the operating pattern of the airline,
such as high number of take-offs and landings. So the actual repairs
and overhauls arising from the engines in service will depend on how
much and in what way they have been used. The market forecast of
business will depend, not only on existing aircraft fleets, but also on
the number of engines being installed in new aircraft.

The share of the market that the business obtains will depend on
geographical location, whether or not the airline has its own repair
base, whether prices can match or undercut those of the competi-
tion, or whether certain types of repair can be done that others
cannot handle. Hanging on to this share of the business will also
depend on how quickly the engine can be turned round in the factory,
from initial inspection to despatch off test. Some other business will
come from carrying out component repair for other repair operations
and from repairing and re-using components out of unserviceable
and scrapped engines that have been purchased.

Having established a diagram of the business operation in this
way, it will then be necessary to decide the scope of the model to be
built. If a strategic or long-term forecast of the business is required
then market strategies and market shares will need to be built in. If,
alternatively, a shorter term view is needed, then the model could
be driven simply by estimates of future repairs arising. In both
models the variables will be defined separately for each engine type
and for each market or customer type.

With an overview of the business operation, as shown in Figure
4.1, it is possible to translate that into a model. It is important at
this stage however that the way the business behaves and interfaces
with its environment is not glossed over, but accurately represented.
Care should be taken to find out the realities of the business and
how things might change in the future, particularly with regard to
market or sales forecasts on which so much of the business plan will
be built.

MODEL OVERVIEW

The business model overview, shown in Figure 4.2, could be regarded as a representation of the way any set of programmed

calculations would be carried out on a computer, whether mainframe or desktop. They would all follow the same pattern. The data variables, which are input and can be changed, would be referenced by the model's calculations to produce the answers. These answers would usually then be output as some form of report.

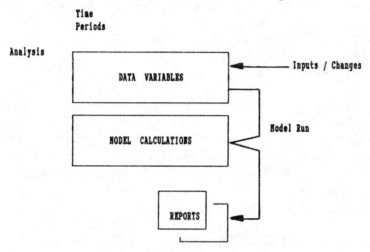

Figure 4.2   Model Overview

Figure 4.2 is intended to represent the actual layout on a desktop-based spreadsheet. The columns of this spreadsheet are the time periods, usually years with this type of model, and the rows relate to the detailed analysis and structure of the model. It is the type of model that could be used to produce long-term forecasts or strategy plans, where calculations are done for all years at the same time and where the range would most likely be from five to fifteen years. This is the type of model we will be looking at in this chapter. In the next chapter we will look at the particular requirements of short-term forecasting models.

The data variables section of this spreadsheet is the area that will accept inputs and changes. The model calculations would first be tested and proved to be giving the correct answers. They would then be protected so that no further changes could be made or no figures could be entered to override them. Having spent a significant amount of time in getting the model right we would not want to have it corrupted.

The outputs from the model could take many forms, but would usually be either a profit statement and balance sheet type of report, or a listing of transactions that could be linked to a spreadsheet reporting system in which reports could be more easily set up and changed. We look at the latter of these options in Chapter 6, where a spreadsheet reporting model is described.

A model set up in this way can be used to try out many different scenarios and options. Changes can easily be made to one or more variables and the model run to calculate revised answers. It can give the answers to 'what happens if ?' and can also be used to optimise the performance of the business.

VARIABLES

The purpose of the business model is to forecast the values of the financial transactions and account balances that enable us to predict the financial performance of the business. The way to forecast transactions is to construct them from the much lower level information on which they depend. How low-level these data variables are depends partly on the nature of the business and partly on the level of detail required in the forecast.

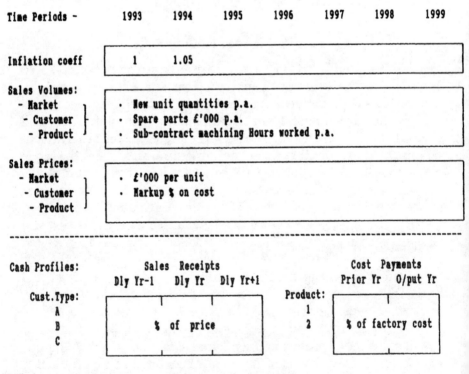

Figure 4.3   Variables

In Figure 4.3 we can see, for example, that sales of new units could be derived from the product of annual quantities and price per unit. The sub-contract machining that is sold, however, would be priced by marking up the cost. So labour cost would need to be calculated first and this would be based on the amount of work done, or hours booked to the job each year. Spare parts sold may not be capable of being forecast in terms of quantities; there may be simply too many to handle. In this case, it may only be feasible to make some prediction of volume by forecasting the sales values of spares each year. These would be valued at base-year levels so that inflation can still be applied quite independently and be changed if required.

The concept of base-year levels is important in a model. If we are to be flexible in the valuation of future business we have to be able to set up inflation rates as variables and perhaps even interest and exchange rates. To apply these rates to calculations they are set up like an index relative to the base year and all variables with financial values are then entered at base-year levels. The base year need not be the first year, but it is advisable to make it as near as possible to current actual levels, so that future forecasts can be based on data that are as accurate as possible. Putting in the values at base-year levels also makes it possible to see where step changes have been made in variables, such as, for example, an expected price increase starting in year 4, perhaps because certain product improvements would command a higher price from then on.

The number of products, customers, or markets to which the variables are analysed again depends on the number of alternatives for each variable and also on the level of detail required in the forecast. There may be, for example, only a few products having different cost structures, but these products may be sold to a very large number of customers with many different terms of business. For the purposes of a strategic plan, it may be possible to simplify such a model by averaging those terms over the different markets, based on past experience. It may, in any case, only be possible to forecast future business levels to markets rather than to customers, so averaging may be essential.

You will see in Figure 4.3 that *Cash Profiles*, which convert revenues and costs into *Receipts* and *Payments*, are not set up across years as are the other variables shown. This is not to say that they never are, but it is counterproductive to input vast amounts of data across years if it remains a constant for each customer type or product. If a profile change is expected at a particular point in time it is usually simpler to treat this as a different product or customer and to set up the other variables separately as well. This has the added advantage of making it possible to phase in an improved or changed product, for example, by using two lines of data, one for the original gradually reducing, and one for the new gradually increasing.

Cash profiles, as you can see, need to reference sales or costs in years both before and after the year of delivery or output. The range of data variables that are set up by years on the spreadsheet will therefore need to allow for this. If sales deposits are called for, or progress payments are made to suppliers in the year before output, then an extra year of data will be required beyond the range of years to be reported. With the sales profiles shown in Figure 4.3, where there are deposits called for in the year prior to delivery (*Dly Yr*-1) and retentions in the year after delivery (*Dly Yr*+1), the range of years calculated and reported could only be from 1994 to 1998 if the first and last years are to have the correct cash receipts and capital employed figures.

The layout of data variables in the spreadsheet can vary with the type of model, but generally it is easier to make changes and re-run the model if the data are near the top and all together. In other models though, it is sometimes better to see the calculated answer change when the variable is changed. In this case the variable is best located alongside the calculations. I deal with these and other considerations of model design in Chapter 8.

BASIC MODEL CALCULATIONS

Having established and set up the data variables, then the calculations of the higher level figures can be constructed in a logical progression down the spreadsheet. Figure 4.4 shows the calculation of a sales line from *Quantity* and *Price* variables. The *Price* data are at base-year levels and there is a step change in price at year *D*, perhaps because of a product improvement. Base year is year *B*, with the *Inflation coefficient* at 1 in this year and the inflation rate at 5 per cent per annum thereafter.

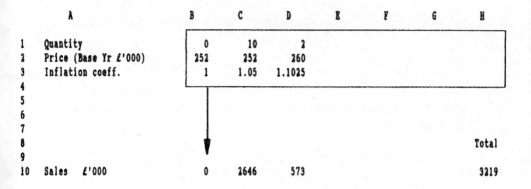

A	B	C	D	E	F	G	H
1 Quantity	0	10	2				
2 Price (Base Yr £'000)	252	252	260				
3 Inflation coeff.	1	1.05	1.1025				
4							
5							
6							
7							
8							Total
9							
10 Sales £'000	0	2646	573				3219

Figure 4.4   Basic Model Calculations

The calculation of *Sales* in year *C* is carried out by the formula:

ROUND(C1*C2*C3)

which indexes the contents of cells $C1$, $C2$ and $C3$ in the data table (namely 10, 252 and 1.05) and multiplies them to give the inflated *Sales* value 2646. This answer comes to exactly 2646, but the answer to *Sales* in year *D* would be 573.3 had the spreadsheet rounding function not been applied to the calculation. It is important that all calculations are rounded into the spreadsheet in this way, otherwise not only will the spreadsheet fill up with decimals, but differences will build up in later figures if they are subsequently rounded. The rounding needs to be done from the first calculation, not at some later stage in the calculation chain. Sales, for example, will form part of the calculation of customer debts, will be part of profits, then will be converted into sales receipts to become part of the bank balance. Ultimate rounding of these secondary numbers could produce an out of balance in the accounts.

There is one thing that spreadsheet users often do, that should be avoided at all costs. Instead of rounding numbers into the spreadsheet as part of the calculation formula, the calculated numbers are formatted. They then appear on the page as rounded numbers, but to the computer are still decimals. The resultant spreadsheet, though looking very authentic, will have vertical totals that do not necessarily agree with the figures shown in each column, and cross totals that may not agree with totals of figures shown in each row. In other words, any figure on the page could be right or wrong.

The *Sales* line in Figure 4.4 has been totalled across using another resident spreadsheet function called SUM. The formula used here is:

$$SUM(B10:G10)$$

which defines within the brackets the range of cells to be added together. The total could have been derived by simply putting in the formula:

$$B10+C10+D10 \ldots +G10$$

but with this type of forecasting model, which might have a range of ten or more years, this formula would have been much longer and time-consuming to enter. There would also have been much more chance of error, such as missing out one reference, for example, which could have been difficult to find later. Changing the range of such a formula when using SUM usually means changing just one cell reference, whereas the other method could mean adding or subtracting several cells, giving a bigger chance of error.

If such simple disciplines are observed in the construction of spreadsheet models then the answers are more likely to be accurate and dependable. The real danger with using computers is that a printout looks very authentic to the unpractised user and decisions significantly affecting the business could be made on the strength of it. If a model is subsequently found to be incorrect the credibility of the business analyst will be shot to pieces.

CALCULATIONS USING SALES PROFILES

The *Receipts Profile* at the top of the Figure 4.5 spreadsheet shows, that for any sale, only 75 per cent is received in the year of delivery, with 15 per cent being received in the year before (*Dly year*-1) and 10 per cent being retained by the customer until the year after (*Dly year*+1). To calculate sales receipts for a particular year, therefore, we have to put a formula in that year, which relates not only to that year's sales, but also to sales in the years either side. To pick up the deposits that will be received in this year we reference next year's sales and to pick up receipts from debts or retentions we look back to last year's sales.

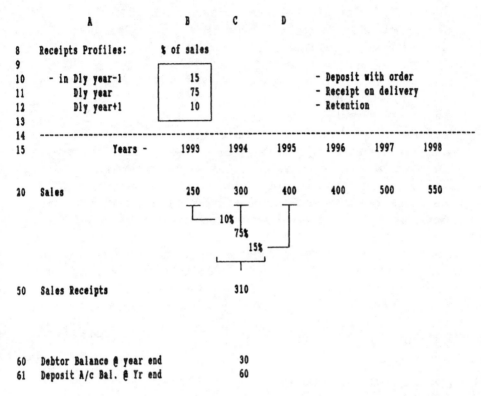

Figure 4.5 Calculations Using Profiles – Sales

The formula that gives the 1994 *Sales Receipts* figure of 310 in Figure 4.5 is:

$$ROUND((B10\%D20)+(B11\%C20)+(B12\%B20))$$

This adds together the 15 per cent *Deposits* from 1995 *Sales*, the 75 per cent against *Deliveries* in 1994 and the 10 per cent retained from *Sales* in 1993. The formula shown for 1994 *Receipts* would be replicated or copied across the other years in order to calculate receipts in all years. The spreadsheet programme would allow for the sales column references of line 20 (*D*, *C* and *B*) to change automatically, but the profile references of $B10$, $B11$ and $B12$ would need to remain fixed, since they relate to all years.

The calculation of *Debtor* and *Deposit Account* balances at the year end can also be made from the same receipts or terms of business profile. The calculation is much simpler than for receipts. The *Debtor* or *Customer Account balance* at the end of 1994 will be the 10 per cent that is held back from 1994 *Sales* and received in 1995. The *Deposit Account balance* at the end of 1994 will be the 15 per cent of 1995 *Sales* received as *Deposits* in 1994.

These calculations appear to be based on a receipts profile that falls clearly into years around the point of sale. However, in the real world things are not usually so straightforward. The receipts will usually fall several months either side of delivery. Even those due on delivery will actually be received on monthly account. The sales value on which the calculation is based is also probably the total of several units or volume of work that would be delivered throughout the year. In this type of long-term forecast it would normally not be practical to phase the sales monthly in order to calculate how many month's sales fell into other years. What has to be assumed is that the sales total for the year is all delivered at mid-year. The monthly based terms of business can then be turned into a percentage profile that puts receipts into other years by counting forwards and backwards around that point. Any deposit, for example, that was contracted to be received less than six months before delivery would remain part of receipts in the delivery year rather than falling into the prior year.

CALCULATIONS USING COST PROFILES

Whereas sales tend to be received in lumps at particular points in time, expenditure on manufacturing the product tends to be incurred continuously over the period of the manufacturing cycle. This expenditure usually follows a cost profile that starts well before delivery with progress payments to suppliers. It builds up to a peak as most parts and sub-contract work comes into the factory and as in-house machining and sub-assembly get going. It then tails off as final assembly and testing complete the cycle.

Such a cycle is shown on the left of Figure 4.6A, where the parts purchase profile has been shown separately so that expenditure on credit from suppliers can be calculated. The timing of *Parts* deliveries and *Labour* bookings extends across quarters prior to our assumed mid-year *Sales Delivery*. In some operations the manufacturing cycle might revolve around an output programme rather than sales delivery, where perhaps it was more cost effective to have a steady labour load than to minimise finished stocks. The *Expenditure* cycles, as you will see, are shown as quarterly percentages of their total cost. Also shown, on the right, are the resultant proportions of *Cost* falling into prior and delivery years. The *Cost Profile*, as a percentage of total cost, is then derived from the prior and delivery year totals. Also shown are the percentages that the cost of parts and labour are to these totals.

Expenditure in Qtrs prior to -						Delivery •	Total Cost	Prior Year: % Cost	Source %	Delivery Year: Cost	Source %
	6	5	4	3	2	1					
Parts s/ctr %	10	2	2	75	11		580	89 516	100	64	33
Labour %					60	40	120	0		120	62
Test %						100	10	0		10	5
							710	516	100	194	100

Prior year | Dly Yr

Total Cost Profile : | 100 % | | 73 % | | 27 % |

Figure 4.6A   Cost Profile Construction

Having established the cost structure and expenditure profile of the product in this way, we can then build the model to calculate the transactions and balances we wish to forecast. The variables, set up near the top of the spreadsheet in Figure 4.6B, are the number of months worth of annual parts purchases that remain unpaid at the end of the year (2 *mths*), together with the proportions of the *Cost Profile* being spent over prior and current years and the *Parts Content* of those proportions, as constructed in Figure 4.6A.

The model calculates *Expenditure* from *Cost of Sales* by reference to the *Cost Profiles*, taking 73 per cent of prior year and 27 per cent of delivery year. The formula for the 1993 figure (2648) is:

$$\text{ROUND}((B10\%C20)+(B11\%B20))$$

The level of *Stock* and *WIP* at year end is calculated by applying the prior year profile percentage (73 per cent) to the next year's *Cost of Sales*. This is because the expenditure on units that will be completed next year will be work in progress at the end of this year. The last calculation shown is the balance due to *Suppliers* at the end of the year, in respect of purchases of parts not paid for. This formula establishes the parts content of expenditure on next year's and current year's cost of sales, then takes the $2/12$ths of this that will be unpaid at the end of the year. The formula, for 1993, is:

$$ROUND((B7/12)*((C10\%(B10\%C20))+(C11\%(B11\%B20))))$$

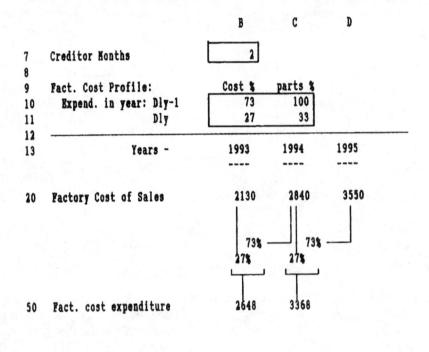

		B	C	D
7	Creditor Months	2		
8				
9	Fact. Cost Profile:	Cost %	parts %	
10	Expend. in year: Dly-1	73	100	
11	Dly	27	33	
12				
13	Years -	1993	1994	1995
		----	----	----
20	Factory Cost of Sales	2130	2840	3550
		73%	73%	
		27%	27%	
50	Fact. cost expenditure	2648	3368	
60	Stock & WIP Bal. @ year end	2073		
61				
62	Supplier Balances @ year end	377		

Figure 4.6B   Calculations Using Cost Profiles

These would not be all the transactions and balances that could be calculated from the cost of sales and variables that have been set up. It does show though, how the model can be built up in an integrated way. It also shows how flexible even this limited model would be. The model could show the profit and cashflow effects of delaying payments to suppliers, buying in parts later, or sub-contracting some of the labour load, simply by changing one or two of the five variables each time.

SWITCHING AND SELECTION

There is one technique that can transform the speed with which a model can react to change and which can turn it into a much more powerful tool for making decisions. This is the use of switches. By definition, switches can turn things on or off, or make and break connections. They can be used in models to do exactly that. In Figure 4.7 there is a switch that can be set either to inflate or not inflate the forecast and other switches further down that can be used to select products simply by switching them in or out.

	A		B	C	D	E	F	G
			Switch	1993	1994	1995	1996	1997
1								
2	Inflation coeff.		1	1	1.05	1.1025	1.1576	1.2155
3		Product:						
4	Quantities:	A	1	5	10	15	20	20
5		B	0	0	1	2	4	6
6								
7	Price:	A		200	200	210	220	220
8		B		300	300	300	320	320
9								
10	Sales:	A		1000	2100	3473	5093	5348
11		B		0	0	0	0	0
12				------	------	------	------	------
13		Total		1000	2100	3473	5093	5348
14				------	------	------	------	------

Figure 4.7 Switching and Selection

The notation used to turn the switch on is a number one and to turn it off a zero. Apart from being a commonly accepted notation in electronics and on electrical equipment, the real reason for this is that it is the simplest way of using such a switch. The switch is used as a coefficient or multiplier in the model, so that multiplying the calculation by one gives the answer to the calculation, but multiplying by zero gives an answer of zero or turns the calculation off.

In the use of such switches, shown in Figure 4.7, the *Inflation* switch has been set to on, and *Product* switches have been set to switch on *Product A* and switch off *Product B*. The calculation in cell C10 multiplies the product switch and the base-year sales value (*Qty x Price*) and then applies inflation, by using an IF statement. The formula is:

$$ROUND(B4*C4*C7*IF(B2=1,C2,1))$$

The logical IF statement says that if the inflation switch is on ($B2=1$) then multiply by the *Inflation coefficient* for the year (in $C2$), otherwise multiply by 1. Multiplying by an inflation coefficient of 1 would leave the sales uninflated, or at base-year levels.

The advantage of this technique is that a model can be set up with the data and calculations required for every possible current and future product or market, then different strategies can very quickly be evaluated simply by changing switches. The switching can also be extended to select such things as product development expenditure options, or to switch different areas of the business in or out of the model. Product switching can also be used to analyse the business in different ways, by running the model with different sections switched in. This overcomes the need to programme complex reports in the model in order to get such analyses. Such reports would be difficult to change or expand.

It obviously helps if such switching is designed into a model initially, because changing a model later not only takes time, but makes it possible for errors to creep in. Having said that, using switches as coefficients makes it as easy as possible to add them later.

MODEL STRUCTURE

A long-term or strategic model does not need a great amount of detail, but it does have to cover a wide timespan. The structure of this type of model therefore allows for all years to be calculated together and gets from profits to cashflow by the least detailed route, by using movements in capital employed.

Figure 4.8 shows this model structure. The size of the model is very largely determined by the number of products and markets that are built in. All the sections within the *Sales & Profits* module, down to and including *Profit contributions*, would all have a common analysis by categories of product and market. So putting in one extra market for a particular product would mean at least six extra lines in the model, counting two for variables (sales quantity and price). Each of these lines could mean up to 15 annual figures, making a total additional space requirement of 90 numbers for each extra category. Space however is not the problem it used to be, nor is the speed of calculation, given the capacity and power of the modern desktop computer. Even so such models would be unlikely to get bigger than 250K, even with about 40 to 50 product/market categories and about 500 lines. The more figures that have to be input though could mean more risk of errors creeping in.

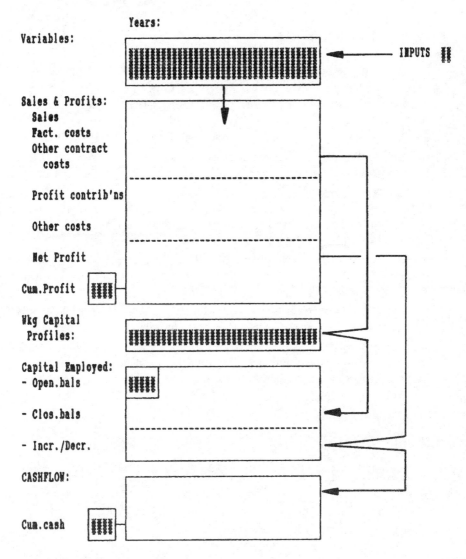

Figure 4.8　Model Structure

In Figure 4.8, the lines with arrows represent the data and calculated figures that are referenced or indexed from one section to another. They also show the general flow of calculations. Inputs and changes are made by the user into the hatched areas, namely *Variables, Working Capital Profiles, Capital Employed, Profit* and *Cash Opening balances*. All other areas would contain calculations and be protected once the model had been built and tested. What are not shown, for the sake of simplicity, are the variable and product switches, which were the subject of the previous section.

The first stages of the model calculate the profit contributions made by each product. This is a very valuable piece of information to have about the business when considering product strategies and ways of optimising profits. To this end, it is important that all products that differ in cost structure, markets, or other variables are defined separately in the model. Too much averaging will obscure the realities of the contributions, or even losses, that products are expected to make.

Getting to a final net profit forecast in the model means deducting from total contributions the other costs, such as development projects, non-product related overheads and interest charges. What are not shown in this diagram are modules that might be included to calculate profits tax and the depreciation and capital allowances required for those taxation calculations.

Capital Employed Closing balances at each year end are calculated by applying the *Working Capital Profiles* to *Sales* and *Cost* values. *Cashflow* is then calculated from *Profit* (before tax) by applying the increases or decreases in *Capital Employed* balances. If taxation calculations had been made, the tax payments forecast would then have been deducted from this cashflow.

TUNING THE MODEL

A model that gives the wrong answers can be a disaster, especially if the user does not realise they are wrong. The way to prove a model, before it is used in anger, is to load it with actual data and run it to calculate answers that are known, such as last year's actuals or the current year's budget. However, it is often easier to use budgeted numbers rather than actuals because data such as unit costs are more likely to be available in the form required for the model. If actuals can be used though, they will be firmer ground than a budget, which may itself be flawed.

The process of proving the model in this way is called tuning because it is necessary to go through a sequence of fine adjustments to get key answers to agree with the known results. This sequence is shown in Figure 4.9, though it is probably not immediately obvious. The overall process entails changing variables in the model (shown within the boxes) so that key numbers are made to agree with actuals. These numbers are agreed in two sequences, first *Profit* in the sequence *A* to *C*, then the *Balance Sheet* in the sequence *1* to *6*.

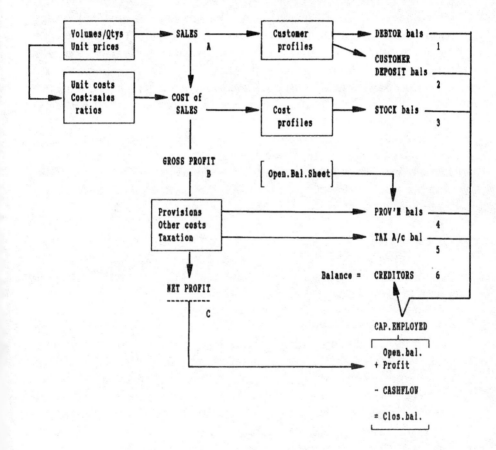

Figure 4.9 Tuning the Model

The first figure that must be agreed is *Sales*. This is tuned by product and market by checking and adjusting *Unit prices* and values of sales for spares or work done. After making changes to data the model is re-run to see how close the sales figures have become. The danger here is that errors will have been corrected that make the total sales come right, but that other product pricing remains unchecked. This could affect product profit contributions in later years when the model is used to produce forecasts, so it is important to check sales on all products. Some sales may be marked up from cost, in which case the relevant ratios would be adjusted to give the correct sales value.

The next figure to correct is *Gross Profit*. This is done by adjusting *Unit cost* variables on products until the *Cost of Sales* is sufficient to give that result. Again it is usually necessary to get the *Gross Profits* to agree on each product, not only to ensure that the total comes out correctly, but also to have a firm base of profit contributions for products that we are going to forecast in the future. Checking and adjusting figures for *Provisions, Other costs* and *Taxation* should then result in a *Net Profit* from the model that agrees with the known result for the test year.

The balances that make up *Capital Employed* are the next figures to be agreed, in the sequence 1 to 6. *Debtors* and *Customer Deposit balances* are corrected by checking and adjusting the *Customer profiles*, which are set up as variables in the model and which reference the previously corrected sales values. *Stock* and WIP balances are similarly corrected by adjusting the profiles that relate to *Cost of Sales*. These profiles, for *Debtors* and *Stocks*, are usually related to markets and product groups, so the tuning process may be a bit time-consuming because actual sales and cost of sales will not necessarily be in that shape to start with.

Getting *Provisions* and *Taxation* to agree in the *Profit account* makes it possible to agree balances on those accounts by changing cash payments. To do this it might be necessary to put in adjustments that override the calculated answers, but the methods of calculating these figures should also be examined and, if found wanting, changed.

You can see from Figure 4.9 that total *Capital Employed* is established from its opening balance by adding the *Profit* from the model and deducting the modelled *Cashflow*. *Creditors* are then the balancing figure that is required to make all the balances total up to *Capital Employed*. The extent to which *Creditors* disagrees with actual balances can be adjusted, partly by tuning supplier payment profiles, but also by manually adjusting cash payments in the test year. The usual problem with actual creditors is understanding what the balance represents in terms of supplier credit and whether it is a normal situation or not. So it is as well to be wary of changing profiles too much simply to get the test year to agree.

When all these tuning adjustments have been made, then the model can be used in earnest in the knowledge that it will behave as expected and produce forecasts that are credible. It is as well, at this stage, to ensure that protection of the model has been completed.

Summary

☐ To model any business it is necessary to chart the external and internal interfaces, so that the flow of work through the business is properly understood.

☐ All business models identify the variables and use them in calculations that produce results in some form of report.

☐ Variables represent the lowest level of information required to calculate results. The form they take will depend on the way the business operates.

☐ Inflation, interest and currency conversions can best be handled by relating their indices to financial variables at base-year values.

☐ Ensuring that spreadsheet calculations are accurate enables trust to be put in the finished model. An inaccurate model is a disaster.

☐ Profiles are relationships that define how sales become receipts and how costs become expenditure and payments.

☐ The use of switches to select and switch on calculations turns a model into a powerful 'what happens if?' tool.

☐ A long-term forecast, or strategic planning, model does not need so much detail and calculates all years simultaneously, with cashflow being derived via capital employed changes.

☐ A model must be fine-tuned to give known answers before it can be used for other forecasts.

Short-term Forecasting

In the last chapter we looked at ways in which the business could be modelled to produce long-term or strategic forecasts. These forecasts cover a wide range of years and the level of detail that could be held as answers in the model was limited. The needs of short-term forecasts are somewhat different. We need to be able to see in much more detail how the business is expected to behave in the near future, so that actions to adjust and change operations by management can be directed at more specific targets.

The type of model used for long-term forecasting would need to be very big to enable it to hold the increased level of detail; so big that it would become too unwieldy and slow in operation. But there is another way. The model can be set up to run one year at a time. The results for that year can then be shown and printed out in much more detail. Another advantage of such a method is that the number of calculations otherwise required for any model run can be significantly reduced by deriving balance sheet figures directly from cashflow. It also means that only the years directly affected by changes need to be run, rather than the whole range of years as in the long-term forecast model.

BASIC MODEL STRUCTURE

To meet the needs of calculating one year at a time the model is structured as shown in Figure 5.1. Data variables are still held for the whole range of time periods (years or shorter periods) and final results and reports are also generated across that range. The detailed calculations within each year though can only be printed out for the year that is run. What this type of model has to come to terms with is the fact that cashflow and balance sheet movements differ from profit by virtue of timing differences. So the cashflow effect of sales and costs cuts across, not only the year being calculated, but also years both before and after. This means that the cashflow and balance sheet effects of each year calculated have to be held by the model and combined with such calculations from other years to produce answers for the full range of years required.

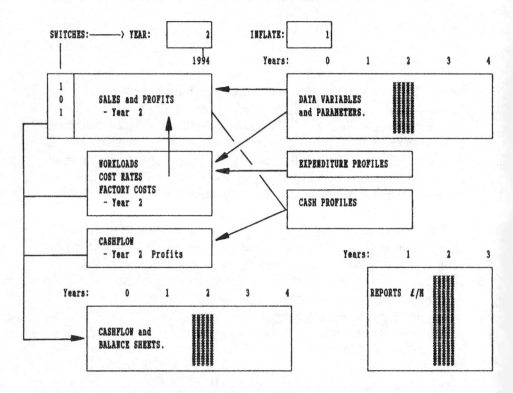

Figure 5.1 Basic Model Structure

It can be seen from Figure 5.1 that this type of model is told what year to run by entering the year reference number (*year 2*). The data variables it needs are then picked up by using this number to index the data tables. *Switches* are also provided for inflation to be applied if required and for any product to be switched in or out. *Sales and Profits* are calculated in detail first, using the product costs generated from a cost module. This module references *Expenditure Profiles*, works out the *Load* in each year and the annual *Cost Rates*. The product costing part of this module is described in a later section of this chapter, but the distribution of expenditure required for cost rate calculations can in itself be a complex process and was covered separately in Chapter 3.

From the sales and cost detail for the year, the *Cashflow* relating to those sales and costs is calculated, also in some detail. To this end, the model references cash receipt and payment profiles. These calculations show how the sales and costs for that year are received and paid in other years as well. As each year is run they build up in slices to total the cashflow across all years. This cashflow build-up also provides the detail required to calculate capital employed balances for all years.

INDEXING DATA

Data tables for short-term forecasting models look much like those used for long-term forecasts, except that the range of years is much less. The difference between the two types of model is the way they use these data. The long-term model uses all years at the same time, but the short-term model indexes only one year at a time.

The key to indexing a single year's data is to give each year a reference, which is the column number of the range of years. This number is then input to a specific cell to make the model run that year and pick up the data column it requires. In Figure 5.2, the data tables are defined by naming them. When such ranges are named in the spreadsheet each cell in that range can be indexed by reference to the column and row offsets for that named range.

The first named range shown in Figure 5.2 is *YEAR*, which contains the year headings. This is used to display the year being run, which appears on reports. The function used to index the year is a built-in spreadsheet function called INDEX, which uses the column and row offsets, namely *B2* containing the column (2) and zero, which is the first, and only, row offset. Column and row offsets of a named range start at zero, so the inflation table will also be indexed with a row offset of zero.

The *Sales Quantity* and *Price* data tables, you will see, each have the same row format, where products are arranged in the same sequence and have been given a *Reference Number*. The reference number is used as a row offset index for those tables and the named ranges have been defined as starting from the row before the first *Product* reference so that references can start at one rather than zero. To index the sales quantity for product *A*, therefore, the formula would use its product reference number, 1, as the row offset of the range *QTYS*.

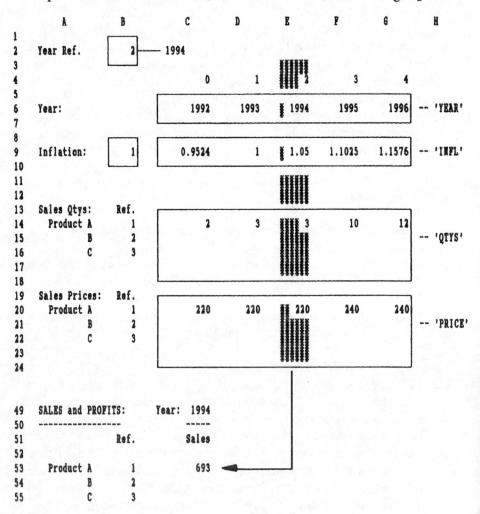

Figure 5.2   Indexing Data

In practice this also makes it possible to analyse the profit statement, for example, in whatever product sequence is required. As shown in Figure 5.2, the product reference entered in cell *B*53 is used in the sales calculation formula to index quantities and price for product *A*. Simply changing the reference number at line 53 would therefore change the calculation of sales to a different product. To make all this work, of course, the data tables must be kept in the same product sequence, so if a new product is added it has to have the same reference in all tables.

The formula for sales in cell $C53$ is somewhat complex and looks like this:

$$\text{ROUND(IF}(B9=1,\text{INDEX(INFL},B2,0),1)$$
$$*\text{INDEX(QTYS},B2,B53)*\text{INDEX(PRICE},B2,B53))$$

This complexity arises from the need to index each variable in the calculation and, if we also had a currency exchange rate and product switches involved as well, it would become even more complex. A good way of making this indexing easier to handle in practice is to index the tables for the year being run into a separate column alongside those tables. The formulae calculating figures such as sales can then simply reference the cells in this column for all the variables needed. Incidentally, this sort of trick cuts down the size of the spreadsheet – it is the big formulae that take up the most space.

SALES RECEIPTS CALCULATIONS

One of the key techniques for running a model year by year is, therefore, the ability to build up the cashflow in annual or periodic slices. Figure 5.3 shows how this is done for sales receipts. The time periods, you will see, are *Quarters* rather than years because this is quite often the need with short-term models. Monthly forecasts are also frequently required, but I would argue that these are less likely to be realistic, particularly for cash forecasts. Actual cashflow cannot be manipulated like profits and comparisons with monthly forecasts will have so many timing variances as to make them useless from the point of view of control. I think a quarter is the shortest time period that has any credibility.

The profile of receipts in Figure 5.3 extends over a range of seven quarters and revolves around the *Delivery Quarter*. As with annual time periods the quarters have been numbered and, clearly, in the real world would represent three years, from the base year onwards. The target year, or the year we wish to forecast, is the middle one of these three. The number of quarters we need in the range either side of this year depends on the number either side of delivery in the profile. In this example we need to start at least with *Qtr 3* to pick up the first 5 per cent retention (22) falling into our target year and to finish with *Qtr 12* to pick up the last front-end deposit (72) in this year. If we wish to use this type of model as a rolling forecast, we can make it move on either by changing the numbers in the quarters to higher numbers, or by changing the base year to which the quarters relate. The first of these options would probably mean adding extra quarters of data, the second would mean replacing most of the data with figures at revised base year values.

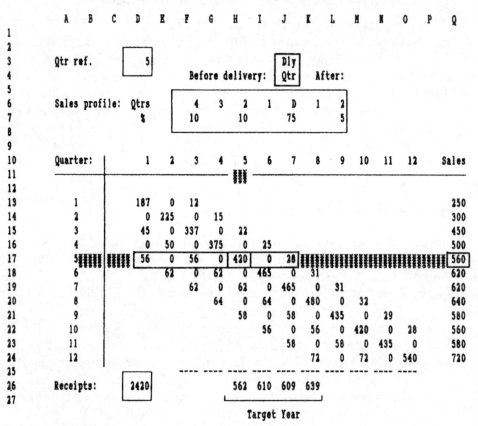

Figure 5.3   Sales Receipts Calculation

In practice, where I have shown the matrix in Figure 5.3 being built up from a single receipts profile, the total receipts from sales in any quarter would relate to many contracts or customers having different profiles. The matrix would then be constructed from slices, which were for the total sales in the quarter to which the separate profiles had been applied. So the receipts slice in the boxes at *Qtr 5* would be the sum of receipts calculated by customer type.

To get the model to put the receipts slice in the right quarter, the quarter being calculated, referenced at cell $D3$, is compared with the quarter down the left side of the matrix. If they are the same then the slice is entered, if not then whatever is in those cells should be left there. So the formula for cell $D17$ is:

$$IF(A17=D3,ROUND(F7\%Q17),D17)$$

which says: if the quarter number of line 17 is equal to the quarter reference at $D3$, then put in the 10 per cent of sales for *Qtr 5*, otherwise leave the figure already in $D17$. This type of statement is usually treated as a circular or simultaneous calculation and the computer iteration count would probably need to be set at a fixed number. We came across this in Chapter 3 when we looked at simultaneous distribution.

Once the model has been run for all quarters total receipts will have been built up for the target year. Subsequent changes to sales in a single quarter will mean running just that quarter to give revised receipts totals, because totals for all quarters are recast each time the model is run. Balance sheet calculations, as you will see shortly, are also derived from receipts and payments, so all calculations can be adjusted by running only the quarters in which sales or cost changes occur.

THE FACTORY COST MODULE

The cost of a product is built up over a period of time, often over more than a year. In a model that runs one year at a time, therefore, expenditure has to be totalled over years (or quarters) in slices, in the same way as receipts in the previous section. The method of calculating expenditure in this way is more complex than for receipts. The different sources of cost not only have different profiles, but they also have to be handled differently depending on whether they are purchases or in-house labour. Purchases of materials and sub-contract labour are defined per unit as monetary values, whereas labour is defined as hours per unit and only gets valued when the process cost rate has been calculated. In Figure 5.4A the *Unit Cost* table can be seen with the *Expenditure Profiles*, namely the percentages of each cost source falling into current and prior years. This example is shown having annual time periods. If quarters had been used then the tables would of course have been extended sideways to accommodate the increased number of columns required.

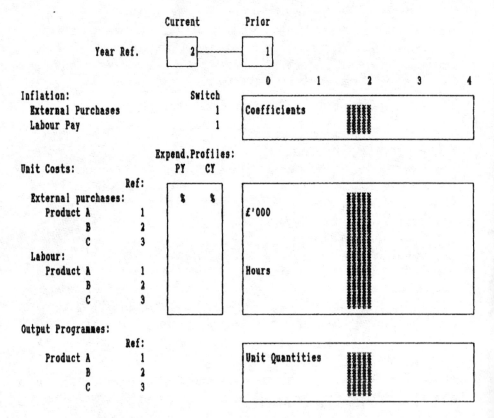

Figure 5.4A Factory Cost Module: Variables

At the very top of the diagram there are two *Year References*. The first of these, the *Current Year*, is input and is the year to be run by the model. The second, the *Prior Year*, is put in by a formula which makes it the current year minus one. These two numbers are used to index the *Inflation* and *Labour Cost* rates that are to be used, and the current year reference alone is used to index the *Output Programme* quantities for the year and to point the expenditure slices to the correct years.

The calculations derived from these variables are shown in Figure 5.4B. *Expenditure* is calculated first for the year indexed (*year 2, 1994*), with *Purchases* in £'000 and *Labour* in hours. Purchases will be inflated to year of spend, that is, either to current or prior year levels. The current and prior year expenditure slices are then indexed into the matrices below, which build up the whole array by years as each year is run on the model. When the labour hour annual totals have been established then the *Cost Rates* for each year can be calculated by reference to the total labour and *Overhead Costs* of the workshop or process area. These costs will have been calculated by the overhead distribution module, which was described in Chapter 3, and they will have been inflated to the year of spend.

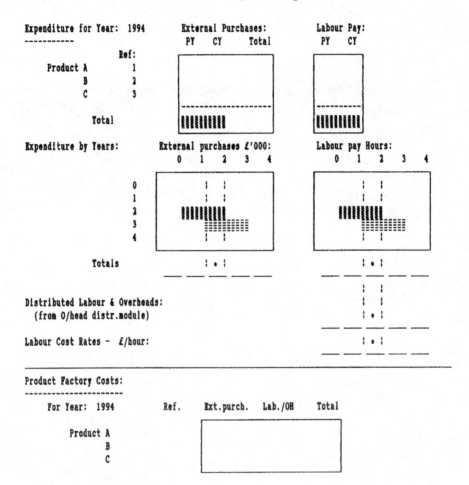

Figure 5.4B   Factory Cost Module: Expenditure and Costs

Finally the total *Product Costs* can be calculated by building up the sources of cost by year of spend. *External Purchases* are derived by addition of prior and current year expenditures for the year being run, which are already in '000's. The labour costs are calculated by multiplying the prior and current year expenditure in hours by the respective cost rates for those years. These costs represent the total output in the year being run and will need to be converted from output to sales levels when calculating cost of sales.

For the sake of clarity in the diagram, I have again omitted the switches that would normally be incorporated for inflation and product selection.

SALES AND PROFITS MODULE

The next set of variables, shown in Figure 5.5A, are those required to calculate sales so that profits can be derived. The diagram itself has been simplified, in that it does not include some of the variables that would normally be set up. In practice there would be an inflation series as part of this calculation, which would be indexed and switched in as required. There could also be an exchange rate for each year set up as a variable, which would be used to convert sales prices that had been set up in a foreign currency.

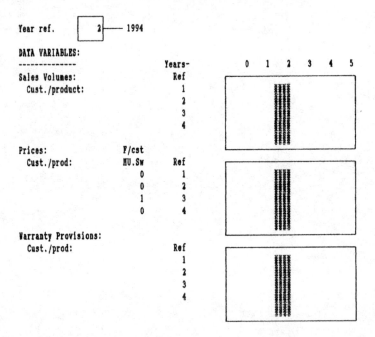

Figure 5.5A Sales and Profits Module: Variables

The sales calculation in fact can be quite complex. The *price data* table in Figure 5.5A shows a column headed factory cost mark-up switch

(*F/cst Mu.Sw*). This is to allow for some customers being cost-plus contracts, where prices are related to, or marked up from, cost. The sales formula would handle this by saying:

IF(f/cost switch=1, take f/cost of this product*m/up in price table, otherwise put in: IF(inflat.switch=1, price in table*inflat.coeff., otherwise price in table))

This ensures that only the fixed price gets inflated and not the price based on a cost that will already have been inflated. If, as is possible, we were also dealing with prices in another currency, there would need to be an additional switch column alongside the price table to indicate whether or not the price was in currency and had to be converted. The formula would then have to deal with this by IF statements as shown above for cost mark-up. The alternative to these complexities is to separate customers and products that are cost-plus or in currency by putting them on their own lines in the data tables and profit statement.

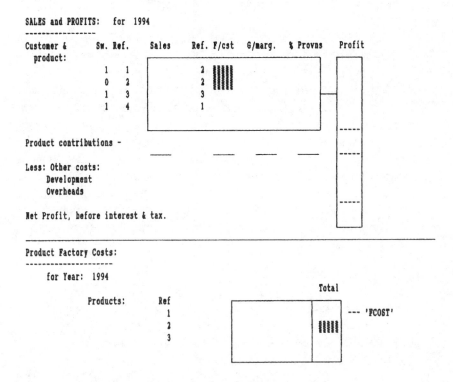

Figure 5.5B   Sales and Profits Module:
Contributions and Net Profit

In the *Sales and Profits* statement, shown in Figure 5.5B, the factory cost value is pulled in against each sales line by putting in a *cost reference number* alongside. This number is then used in the *Factory Costs* formula to index the total cost for these sales from the total column of the *Product Factory Costs* in the cost module, which has been given the range name *FCOST*. To get from output levels to sales levels this cost value is divided by output quantities and multiplied by sales quantities. This method of indexing costs allows for the disparity in numbers between sales customer/product categories and types of product cost. It also allows for the possibility of substituting a cost from a different source, such as buying it rather than making it, simply by changing the reference.

Sales related provisions are charged against the *Gross Margins*, usually by indexing percentages of sales that have been set up in a data table. In this example, warranty provisions have been allowed for and there could well be others. A balance is then struck on each customer/product line to show the contract margins or contributions.

Other costs to be charged below the line, such as *Development* and *Overheads*, would be set up as data tables at base-year levels across the range of years and given range names. The figures for each year would then be indexed into the *Profit* statement and inflated if the inflation switch was on. These costs could also be separately switched in or out on the profit statement if required. In addition, the data table for *Development*, for example, could be set up in more detail by projects, which could themselves be switched in or out of a total at that stage in the model. The way these sorts of options were handled would depend on the tunes to be played on the model. As much flexibility as possible should be built into a model like this because more answers rather than less are always required afterwards.

SALES BALANCES AND TRANSACTIONS

The assertion on which this, and the next two sections, are based is that transactions and balances can both be derived from a common cash or expenditure profile. In this section we are going to deal with sales transactions. Figure 5.6 shows a matrix built up from quarterly slices of sales receipts. It also highlights the *Qtr.5* position and the way in which transactions in this quarter and the balances at the end of the quarter can be derived from this matrix.

```
         A    B    C    D    E    F    G    H    I    J    K    L    M    N    O    P    Q
1
2
3    Qtr ref.        5                              Dly
4                              Before delivery:     Qtr    After:
5
6    Sales profile: Qtrs        4    3    2    1    D    1    2
7                     %        10        10        75        5
8
9
10   Quarter:        1    2    3    4    5    6    7    8    9   10   11   12    Sales
11   ─────────────────────────────▓▓▓─────────────────────────────────────────
12
13     1            187    0   12        D                                        250
14     2              0  225    0   15                               F            300
15     3             45    0  337    0   22                                       450
16     4              0   50    0  375    0   25                                  500
17     5▓▓▓▓▓   B    56    0   56    0  420   0   28                    E    ▓▓▓▓▓ 560
18     6                  62    0   62    0  465    0   31                         620
19     7                       62    0   62    0  465    0   31                    620
20     8                            64    0   64    0  480    0   32               640
21     9                                 58    0   58    0  435    0   29          580
22    10                                 56    0   56    0  420    0   28          560
23    11              C                   A        58    0   58    0  435    0     580
24    12                                           72    0   72    0  540          720
25                   ──── ──── ──── ──── ──── ──── ──── ──── ──── ──── ──── ────
26   Receipts:                          562  610  609  639
27
```

CUSTOMER DEPOSITS & PP's:
A. Receipts in Qtr   120
B. Offsets against sales in Qtr   112
C. Balances at Qtr end   370

CUSTOMER DEBTS:
D. Ledger receipts in Qtr   442
E. Sales billings in Qtr   28
F. Balances at Qtr end   53

Figure 5.6 Sales Balances and Transactions

The total receipts in *Qtr.5*, as we saw in Figure 5.3, are the total at the bottom of the *Qtr.5* column (562). This is made up of two components. The receipts within box *D* comprise 420, which is the receipts on delivery of *Qtr.5* sales, together with a final 5 per cent retention received in respect of *Qtr.3* sales. Both of these are therefore customer ledger receipts in the quarter, as would be any more that fell within this box. Box *A* below, though, captures the receipts in the quarter that are in advance of future sales, namely deposits from customers.

If we now look at the quarter along the horizontal axis, box *B* contains *Customer Deposits* and *Progress Payments* that were received in prior quarters and are now being offset against the sales value in this quarter. In other words, it is the transaction that reduces the amount now due from the customer and clears the deposits previously held. Box *E* is the total of *Sales Billings* not received in the quarter, net of the deposits offset in box *B*. Box *E* is therefore the input to customer debt in the quarter.

The total within box *F* includes the current quarter's debt increase in box *E* as well as retentions from sales in prior quarters that are not yet received (25). Box *F* is therefore the balance of customer debt at the end of *Qtr.5*. Box *C*, in the same way, contains the balance on customer deposits A/c at the end of the quarter, being made up of current quarter receipts in box *A* and other receipts in prior quarters that have not yet been cleared against sales billings.

The transactions and balances *A* to *F* can therefore be derived by totalling all figures within the respective boxes, using the spreadsheet function:

SUM (from top left cell to bottom right cell)

These formulae will be replicated or copied across the time periods (quarters or years).

PURCHASES AND STOCK AND WIP BALANCES

In this section we are concerned with purchased expenditure which, as you can see in Figure 5.7, is profiled over the four quarters before output and into the quarter after. The expenditure slices have been put together in the quarterly matrix and the total purchases invoiced by suppliers in *Qtr.5* are shown at the bottom of that quarter's column (457).

The purchases within box *A* are the inputs to stock during *Qtr.5*, being made up of parts invoiced prior to output in future quarters, plus the 5 per cent invoiced in output *Qtr.5* (20). The outputs from stock in the quarter are totalled into box *B* and again include the 20 at cell *H17*, which is both received into stock and output from stock in *Qtr.5*.

The output costs within box *E* (20) are the 5 per cent of purchases that are invoiced after the output quarter. These will have been accrued into cost at *Qtr.5* and added into the balance of these accruals (or purchase reserve) at the end of *Qtr.5*, which is totalled within box *F*. It follows that the 17 within box *D* would have been accrued in this way in the prior quarter and is now coming out of the balance, being offset or replaced by supplier invoices in the quarter.

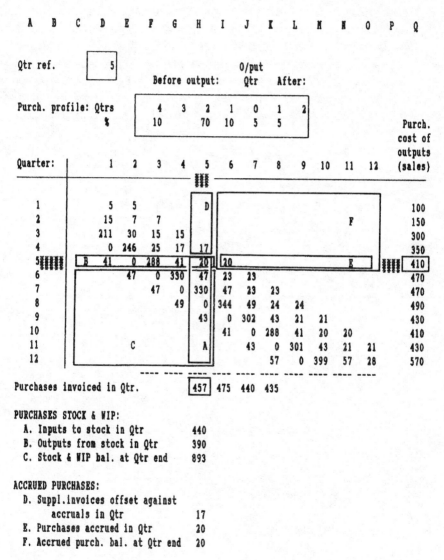

Figure 5.7   Purchases and Stock and WIP Balances

SUPPLIER PAYMENTS AND BALANCES

The totals of purchases invoiced in each quarter have been taken from the matrix in the previous section (Figure 5.7) and profiled in Figure 5.8 to reflect the way these are paid for. Again the slices for each quarter have been built up in this matrix so that the total paid to suppliers in the quarter can be extracted at the foot of each column (455 in *Qtr.5*). The assumed average payment period by suppliers of six weeks has been turned into a profile which says that, of the current quarter's purchase invoices, six of the thirteen weeks' worth will not be paid until the next quarter (0.462) and seven of the thirteen weeks' worth will be paid in the current quarter (0.538).

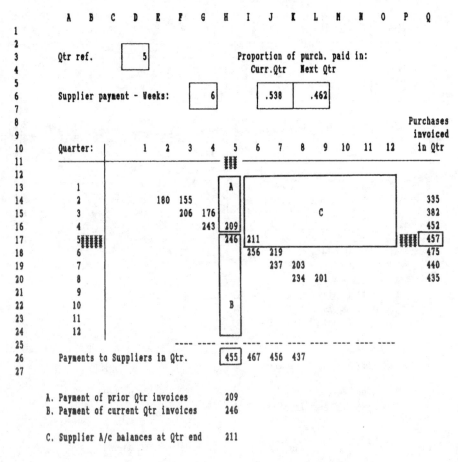

Figure 5.8   Supplier Payments and Balances

It is the invoices paid in the next quarter that form the *Supplier A/c balances* in box *C* (211 at *Qtr.5*). Those that were in the balance last quarter become payments in this quarter, in box *A* (209). Also falling into payments this quarter are invoices received prior to six weeks before the end of *Qtr.5*, in box *B* (246).

ANALYSIS IN REPORTS

The outputs or reports from a model like this need to be quite flexible. It is rarely possible when building the model to know what all the requirements might be over its lifespan. There are really only three ways of generating reports:

1. By adding the various figures together by formula on the line of the report, referencing them by their cell coordinates.
2. Creating a database from all the figures to be analysed and using the functions available with this facility more easily to index them and add them together.
3. Setting up the figures to be analysed as a listing, which is in a format designed to interface with a separate spreadsheet reporting system.

The last of these makes it possible to have several models, for separate parts of the business, for example, reported in the same way, or consolidated. Comparisons can also be made with actuals or other forecasts. Building and using such a reporting system is fully explained in Chapter 6. The other two methods are both ways of producing reports on the face of the model spreadsheet and allow the model to be self-contained.

The first method is effective enough and not too difficult to program initially. When changes are required, or the spreadsheet is altered, then it becomes difficult and time-consuming to rebuild the reports. It can be the best method if the figures that have to be pulled together into the reports cannot be easily formed into a database, or if the reports are very limited in content. If the spreadsheet has been designed with the reporting requirements in mind and the results of calculations are set out within a table or a common range of columns, then the database approach is preferred.

Figure 5.9 shows how analysis using a database works. The table with the columns of figures to be used is named as the *INPUT* range.

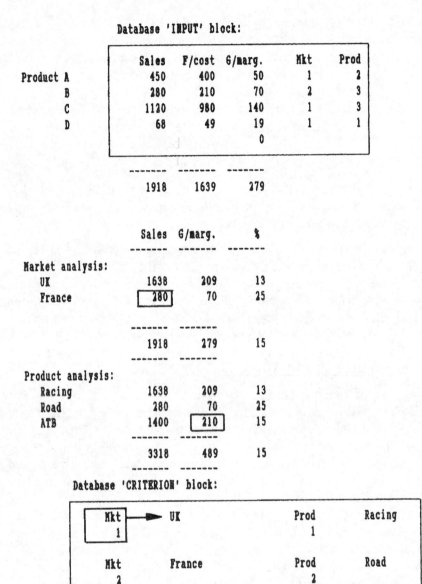

Database 'INPUT' block:

	Sales	F/cost	G/marg.	Mkt	Prod
Product A	450	400	50	1	2
B	280	210	70	2	3
C	1120	980	140	1	3
D	68	49	19	1	1
			0		
	-------	-------	-------		
	1918	1639	279		

	Sales	G/marg.	%
	-------	-------	-------
Market analysis:			
UK	1638	209	13
France	280	70	25
	-------	-------	
	1918	279	15
	-------	-------	
Product analysis:			
Racing	1638	209	13
Road	280	70	25
ATB	1400	210	15
	-------	-------	
	3318	489	15
	-------	-------	

Database 'CRITERION' block:

Mkt 1	→	UK		Prod 1	Racing
Mkt 2		France		Prod 2	Road
				Prod 3	ATB

Figure 5.9   Analysis in Reports – Using a Database

This range will also include columns which are to be used for the selection references called *CRITERIA* and will have a first row that has the criterion names at the head of those columns. As you will see in Figure 5.9, there are to be two analyses provided, by market (*Mkt*) and by product (*Prod*).

The definition of which numbers will relate to the different markets (*UK* and *France*) and to the different products (*Racing, road* and *ATB* (All Terrain Bikes) mountain bikes) are then established within the criterion range. This range of cells should be kept away from, preferably below, the main model so that model line changes do not corrupt it and make it necessary to set it up again. Within this range, the criterion category numbers are given names. In the example *Mkt 1* is named *UK*. Putting a one in the *Mkt* column of the input block will then define figures on that line as being UK market.

To produce an analysis that will aggregate figures in the same categories a data management function DSUM can then be used. This indexes a column of the input range and adds together the figures that have the same criterion name. The market analysis of sales to France (280), for example, has the cell formula:

DSUM(INPUT,0,France)

where the zero is the input block column offset for sales. The product analysis of *G/margin* on ATB bikes (210) has a formula of:

DSUM(INPUT,2,ATB)

where the 2 indexes the G/marg. column of INPUT. The use of the database in this way makes it easy to add new products, new or changed criteria, or new reports without requiring major surgery on the model.

TUNING NOTES

Tuning a short-term forecast is very similar to the procedure outlined in the previous chapter. The main difference lies in the much greater detail built in, which means a more laborious process of checking all the products and customers, so that sales and factory costs work out properly. The factory costs themselves are the result of a chain of calculations that include workloads, numbers of people, pay, overheads and cost rates. So there are a significant number of areas to check if costs do not conform to actual experience.

It is difficult to lay down rules for tuning a model, particularly a short-term forecast model, because every business is different and future operations are not necessarily like past operations. The real keys to building a good model lie in an understanding of the way the business operates and in an acceptance that a model to predict the future will inevitably be something of a compromise, rather than an exact science.

SUMMARY

☐ The need for greater detail in a short-term forecast can be met by a model that runs one year (or quarter) at a time.

☐ Data tables are indexed into calculations by setting them up as named ranges and selecting the year required by reference to the column number. Product/customer categories are defined by the row numbers in each table. Related tables are given common row references.

☐ Cash receipts and payments are built up in slices from sales and costs, as each year is run.

☐ The matrix that builds up sales receipts also generates the customer debt and deposit transactions and balances.

☐ The factory cost module builds up expenditure into a matrix for each source of cost, calculates labour cost rates and evaluates the product costs of sale. These matrices also produce the stock, work in progress and accrued purchases transactions and balances. Supplier invoice values, calculated by the purchases expenditure matrix, are profiled into another matrix to give supplier payments.

☐ The sales and profits module builds up an annual (or quarterly) profitability statement, indexing costs from the cost module. Net profit is derived after calculating and deducting other costs and provisions.

☐ If the results of calculations can be formed into a database, reports can be more easily structured and changed.

6

Reporting Results

For decisions to be taken in a business, financial forecasts have to be presented in a commonly understood form and are usually compared with past results and budgets. Very often a package of reports is required, covering many aspects of the business or project. A system for reporting such results must be able to put many numbers into the right places over a range of different reports. The reports themselves also have to be capable of being reshaped or increased in number and the data that goes into them must be capable of being changed and updated. All this has to happen quickly so that the business can have its results and forecasts as soon as possible and be able to take action to correct any adverse or potentially damaging trends.

Most computer generated reports are part of mainframe-based accounting or book-keeping systems, which tend to be inflexible and are only a printout in the form of the detailed books of account. More presentable customised reports are often produced on PC spreadsheets, wordprocessing, or other software packages, but invariably they are simply a means of entering numbers into reports at the keyboard and printing them out. These PC-based reports overcome the problem of being able to change data, but are prone to inaccuracy. They also tend to be difficult to produce quickly. The accountants not only need a balanced set of accounts before they can be sure the numbers are right, but they have to understand where each number should go and whether it should be positive or negative on the report page. Comparisons of actuals with budgets and forecasts are often difficult because they are rarely produced to the same level of detail.

My solution to this has been to build reports that have programmed instructions to point the numbers into the right places on the page and to have inbuilt controls so that totals that should agree do so. The system that I am going to describe, which is shown in overview in Figure 6.1, has its pedigree in a mainframe system that I built to produce consolidated reports for the Rolls-Royce Group and the reports required by each business within the Group. The ideas and techniques were adapted to spreadsheet use to produce a similar consolidation and reporting system for the five separate sites covered by the Repair Business of the Group at that time.

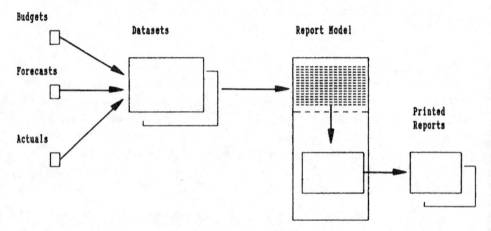

Figure 6.1   Reporting System

You can see an overview of such a system in Figure 6.1. The numbers required for reports are entered into spreadsheets called datasets, which can then be loaded into a report model spreadsheet, which in turn produces the reports for printing. The essential features of the system are that the datasets would be separate spreadsheets, but all having the same data format. They would be saved whenever changes or inputs had been made. The report model, on the other hand, would be initialised with zeros, and after all reports had been printed it would not be saved but zapped from the computer's memory. In this way, although a library is maintained of all the dataset versions, storage space is not cluttered by the reports, which would only be produced and printed on demand.

There can also be different report models, each designed to work with its own matching datasets. Probably the most powerful feature of such a system is its ability to produce consolidated reports from any number of datasets. In addition, the facility to change reports easily makes the system very flexible and simple to maintain.

DATASET STRUCTURE

A dataset, as shown in abbreviated form in Figure 6.2, is a listing of all the transactions and balances that are required for a particular set of reports. The list is usually easier to handle if it is in the sequence shown, namely *Profit a/c details, Balance Sheet* details, and so on, but this is by no means essential. The level of detail is determined by the reporting requirements. Once the list has been established and the report model has been built, then the sequence and narrative of each line cannot be changed easily. The way to make additions is to leave spare lines when the dataset is designed, which can subsequently be used for new or subdivided data.

Company 'A'   £'000

Data Ref.	3	Mth.	2	,1993	Y T D			FULL YEAR	
				Ref.	Actual	Budget	F/cast	Budget	Last Yr
Sales by market:				1					
UK				2					
France				3					
				4					
				5					
Sales by product:				6					
Racing				7					
Road				8					
ATB				9					
Profit A/c detail									
Closing Bal.Sheet A/cs									
Cash receipts/payments									
Fixed Asset movements									
Expenditure detail									
Numbers of people									
Hours worked									

Figure 6.2   Dataset Structure

The narrative itself needs to be designed with the report model in mind because, as we shall see later, it is possible to index lines of text into a report as well as numbers. So the line, for example, that says *France* might have been better entered as *Sales - France* so that it could be taken separately to a report. This makes for considerable repetition in the data descriptions, but the reports themselves can be more flexible and easier to build and change. Self-contained data descriptions are more mobile and can be indexed on their own without losing their meaning. You will see that there are no totals allowed for, total sales for example. These are built up by the report model, as we shall also see later. The dataset needs to contain only what I call primary data, the lowest level of data that has to be input.

At the top of the dataset in Figure 6.2 you will see two numbers in boxes, namely *Data Ref.* and *Mth.* The dataset reference is a permanent part of each dataset. It defines to the system what company or reporting unit the dataset refers to and is used by the report model to recognise what data it is dealing with. In this particular dataset, therefore, *Data Ref.3* relates to *Company A.* The *Mth* is the reporting period and is entered whenever the year-to-date (*YTD*) figures are changed to a later period. It can equally well be quarters, or other accounting periods, if that is the way reports are to be produced. This number can be used by the report model to ensure that the report clearly says what month or period is being reported. Alongside each line of narrative another reference number appears, starting with number one at the first line. These numbers identify each line of data to the report model and are used to index the figures and narrative into reports.

The numeric columns to the right of the dataset in Figure 6.2 will include whatever is to be reported, but the *Last Yr* column may be there only to provide an opening balance sheet, so that reports such as a funds flow statement can be constructed. Full year budget and last year numbers will only need to be input once, usually at the start of the year. Annual forecasts would be input or changed at whatever time a new forecast was prepared. Only the YTD numbers would need to be input each month in this dataset and, as I will show in the next section, even the YTD budget numbers need only be input once in the year. So in operation, the system can require only one column of inputs each reporting period.

The conventions that need to be applied to the form of the data are sometimes alien to accountants who think in terms of double-entry.

What we are dealing with is simply a list of numbers, which are normally all positive and which are added or subtracted on each report page by the report model. The only occasions when numbers are entered in the dataset as negatives are when they are reverse transactions, such as sales returns, or if they represent a reduction or release of a provision rather than an additional provision. In the latter case, the narrative would need to read: provision increase (decrease), in order to tell the user how to enter the number, as positive or negative.

Balances can sometimes be one way or the other, such as Customs & Excise VAT a/c, or a subsidiary company balance. There are two ways to handle these, either by having a line in both debtors and creditors and entering the numbers accordingly, or by having one line in, say, debtors and entering a negative number if it is the reverse. The first is probably more correct in accounting terms, but the latter method has the advantage of having all the columns of that balance alongside each other so that visual comparisons can be made more easily in the dataset.

BUDGET SELECTION

I said in the previous section that it was possible for the YTD budget numbers to be entered only once a year, rather than each month. Figure 6.3 shows how this can be done. Most budgets are phased into months or quarters at the time they are prepared, or when they have been approved. If this is the case, the whole phased set of transactions and balances can be entered into the dataset, to the right of the normal columns of data.

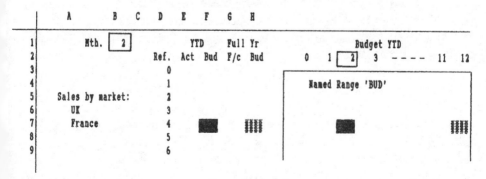

Figure 6.3   Dataset: Budget Selection

In order that the current month's YTD budget numbers can be indexed by the report model, they have to be put into the *YTD Bud.* column (Column *F* in Figure 6.3). To achieve this the phased budget numbers are created as a named range, say *BUD*, which has the month numbers across the top. This named range can then be indexed by reference to the column number that is the same as *Mth* (2) and the line number that is in the data line reference column (*D*). As each month's results are input and the Mth reference is changed, so the corresponding YTD figures will be picked up.

There is a reduced risk of errors by doing things this way, because they are not as likely when data are entered across 12 columns as they are when entries are made each month into a single column. There can also be a much faster reporting time when only actuals have to be entered each month. The budget numbers will have been entered in the early part of the year and outside the peak reporting times.

FORECASTING MODEL INTERFACE

We have seen in a previous chapter that results from a forecasting model can either be embedded in dedicated reports as part of the model, or obtained through an interface with an external reporting system. Numbers can be extracted from the model and entered into the reporting system dataset manually, but the time taken and the risk of error do not make this the best way. Having an electronic interface between the model and the report system dataset is the most accurate way and is one that makes it possible for the dataset to be updated easily when forecasts are changed.

The requirement for this to take place, shown in Figure 6.4, is to have the results from the model listed as transactions and balances, in the same format as in the dataset. Each line of this listing will index the numbers it needs from the body of the forecasting model. If a range of years is to be reported for the forecast, then the whole array, or matrix, of results can be loaded into the dataset. If only a single year is to be used, say for a current year's estimate, then only that year's column can be loaded by using a *part load* command to select it and to define where it is to go in the dataset.

An important part of this loading of numbers from a forecasting model is to specify that only values will be loaded rather than the formulae that make up the array. If formulae are loaded they will result in error messages the instant calculation is carried out; they are designed to work with references in the forecasting model and not in the report model. Another requirement for the system to work properly, is for the data list in the forecasting model to remain unprotected, so that this protection does not carry across to the report model dataset and from there into the report model. If that were to happen the report model could not be initialised with zeros when required, which as we shall see later, is an important part of the sequence of operations needed to run the report model for certain types of report.

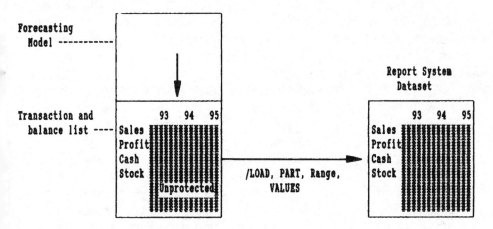

Figure 6.4 Data Interface with Forecasting Model

Using an interface such as this means that any forecasting model, or indeed any model, can be presented through the reporting system in a uniform way and with comparisons with other figures. The only requirement is that the results to be reported, however brief, are listed in the same form as the reporting system dataset. Custom-built reports can then be created, if required, much more quickly within the report model.

DATA CONSOLIDATION

A number of datasets can be added together by carrying out the command to /load,consolidate each dataset in turn to the report model, so that consolidated reports for a group of companies can be produced. In order that a proper consolidation can be prepared, the datasets need to identify separately inter-company sales, balances and other amounts that have to be eliminated from profit, balance sheet and cash to show the group results.

The consolidation can be achieved in either of two ways. The first is by adding the datasets together with the /load,consolidate command, then designing the reports to eliminate the inter-company transactions and balances. This method can be effective if the consolidation is straightforward, but can become rather difficult to understand if a significant number of adjustments need to be made. The other way is to create another dataset to which the consolidation adjustment entries are made, with explanatory notes, and which can be included in the sequence of /load,consolidate commands. There is then a clear audit trail in the conventional way and separate reports can be generated that show the consolidation adjustments made to each line, simply by loading the adjustments dataset on its own.

This ability to consolidate accounts on such a reporting system is a very powerful attribute and was a driving force in my development of these systems. Working out some of the adjustments required takes no less skill than before, but the mechanics of producing consolidated reports is then almost instantaneous. In practice it helps if the company datasets are added together by /load,consolidate as a first stage, so that reports can then be printed in an unconsolidated form. These reports are then a great help in establishing some of the adjustments that have to be made, such as total inter-company sales and balances. Once the adjustments have been worked out and put into the separate dataset, then a full consolidation can be made. This method is almost mandatory if a large number of companies is involved.

You will see in Figure 6.5 that the *Dataset Ref. numbers* are also added together as the datasets are consolidated in sequence. This serves as a log that shows what stage the consolidation has reached and the consolidated ref. number can be used by the report model to identify and index consolidated numbers. The numbers used for each dataset reference are selected so that the stage of the addition sequence can be derived. If *A Company* and *B Company*, for example, had been consolidated the ref. number in the report model would have been 8, and only that combination would give an 8. Using the reference numbers in this way, different parts of a group can be consolidated and reported as well as the total group.

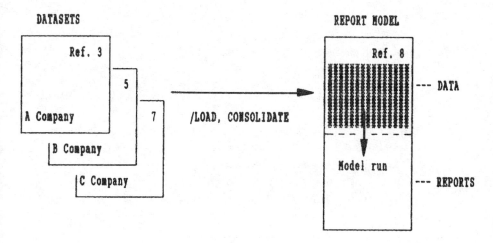

Figure 6.5   Data Consolidation

THE REPORT MODEL

The report model is primed with data from the datasets and is programmed to produce reports from this data. The datasets though, you will recall, hold only the primary or low level data, so any secondary numbers such as totals or sub-totals are constructed within the report model, making them available for use in reports as well. Figure 6.6 shows an overview of a report model, with the dataset being loaded into the primary data area above the dotted line. This area is a copy of the dataset, with all line descriptions and columns being the same.

Before loading the first dataset with /load,consolidate, the numeric area has to be initialised with zeros. This ensures not only that the area is numeric so that the dataset file and report spreadsheet numeric areas get added together, but also that no data remains from a previous report run where the model had been saved instead of being zapped. For similar reasons the cell containing the dataset reference number (not shown in Figure 6.6) also needs to be initialised with zero so that it is not corrupted and shows the true consolidated number.

The size of the secondary data area will depend on the requirements of reports. If summary or total numbers are to be used in reports, such as sales, profit, net cashflow, capital employed, etc., then these will need to be constructed by formula from the primary data numbers (or from other secondary numbers). These secondary numbers can also be used as controls to check on the validity or balance of data being used. As an example of this process:

☐ Sales would be totalled
☐ Net profit would be calculated from sales less costs and provisions
☐ Capital employed (CE) would be calculated by adding detailed asset balances and deducting detailed liability balances
☐ Cash receipts less payments would give a net cashflow figure
☐ This net cashflow figure would then be compared with opening CE plus profit for the period minus closing CE, which should be the same answer.

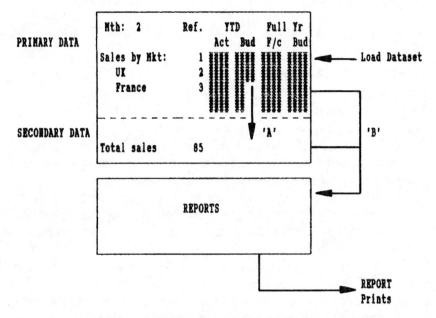

Figure 6.6   Report Model Structure

Other reconciliations would also need to be built into these secondary numbers to ensure that reports came from a balanced set of accounts. As an example, a comparison would be made of changes in fixed asset balances with the net of fixed asset cost movements and the depreciation charge to profit account. Problems start where totals struck on reports do not agree with the equivalent secondary number totals, but I shall discuss such rounding problems later in this chapter.

When the report model is run, by calculating the spreadsheet, the secondary numbers get created and the reports index the data they need from both primary and secondary areas. To complete the run, the reports can then be printed, either together or selectively. Then, after all reports required have been printed, the report model spreadsheet is zapped from memory, leaving a blank model on disk ready to be loaded for another run.

INDEXING DATA

The central feature of the reporting system is the way that data are pointed or indexed into the reports. It makes it possible to create or change reports very easily, it allows formulae in reports to be common to all reports and it allows the user to see where data lines and columns are going to be entered on the report.

Figure 6.7 shows how data is indexed into reports. The upper part of the report model, containing the primary and the secondary data, is given range names, *DESC* for the line description and *DATA* for the numeric columns. The line offset to index each of these is the *Line Ref.number*. The column offsets for the numeric data have been put in above the range for convenience and the column offset for the descriptions will be zero, because there is only one column (*A*). To the right of the report model proper, is a vertical list of the names of the months, which again has been given a range name, *MTH*. From these named ranges it is possible to index data descriptions and numeric values using the range offsets and, also, to index the month that is being reported by using the month number at cell *B*1 for the line offset of MTH.

In the report (*Report A* in Figure 6.7) the column and line offsets of the numeric data and descriptions required are entered slightly outside the top and right-hand borders of the report, that is, just outside the range to be printed out. The formulae in the report body that index the data values and descriptions refer to these offsets, rather than indexing the data area directly. The month name is picked up into the report by reference to the month number cell B1, which indexes MTH as I said before.

You will see that in column *L*, also alongside the report, there is a switch against each line that is either positive or negative. These switches are entered by the user to define whether the values on each line are to be added or subtracted because, as you will recall,

all numbers start out as positive numbers in the dataset unless they are defined otherwise. The switches are used as coefficients either to negate the value or to leave it positive.

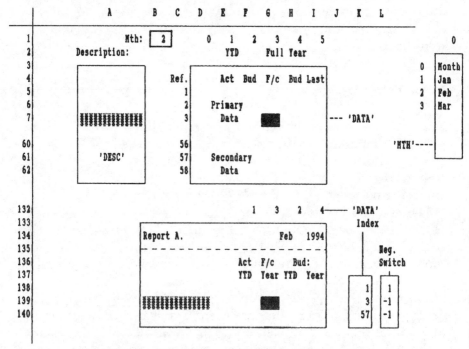

Figure 6.7   Report Model: Indexing Data

The formulae in the report can therefore be common to all reports because they use the offsets alongside to index data. The report content or style can also be very easily changed, simply by changing these offsets and the negation switches.

REPORT FORMATS

Due to the flexibility that the user has available to change the shape of reports, a combination of several different formats is possible within a single report model. However, it clearly makes sense to have a common data format for a set of reports, simply to make them easier to read. A separate report model is also required if the data content is different, as would be the case if we wanted to report the results of a five-year forecast by years, for example.

Figure 6.8 shows some sample layouts of different types of report. On the left is a monthly report for the current year, which has the data column layout that I've been using to demonstrate data structure in this chapter. In the centre is a page reporting a sales forecast over five years, with two different analyses of the same figures. On the right is a report that is rather different. It is a page containing consolidated profit numbers, it also shows them separately by companies within the group.

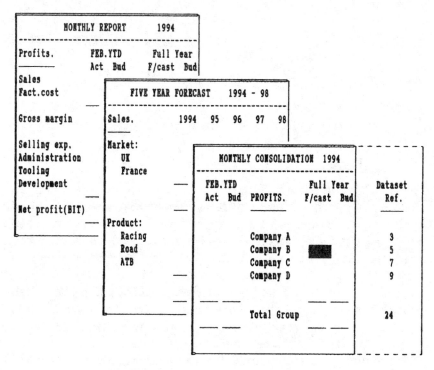

Figure 6.8 Report Formats

A report such as this last one is constructed by first putting alongside the report the dataset reference numbers of the figures that are to go on each line. The datasets for each company are then loaded in sequence, with the model being calculated after each load and initialised before the next load. The formula in each cell of this report will say:

IF the dataset reference of the data that has been loaded is the same as the ref. on this line alongside the report, then enter the value indexed, otherwise leave whatever value is already in the cell.

In this way each company line is entered in turn. When they are done, a full consolidation is done of all the datasets together. The consolidated totals get entered in the report lines, which this time, have a dataset ref. that is equal to the consolidated ref. number (24 in Figure 6.8). This means there can be report pages that have consolidated numbers and those that have separate company numbers, all generated by the same report model.

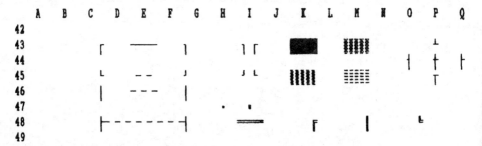

Figure 6.8A   Report-building Character Set

It is useful, when constructing the framework of the first report, to have a set of the characters required somewhere near the bottom of the model. In Figure 6.8A I have reproduced the character set used to construct the diagrams in this book, most of which can be used to build reports. They are ASCII characters that have been generated at the keyboard. A report framework can be very quickly constructed if these are set up on the model, copied to the cells required and then replicated into other cells. Once there is one framework for a common set of reports, then many more can quickly be copied. Where data is indexed by reference to named range offsets then the whole report, including its formulae, can be copied to create others, before putting in the individual report index references.

REPORT SELECTION

More often than not, the intention is to print out all of the reports created in a model together. This can be achieved simply by defining the output range that covers the part of the spreadsheet containing these reports. However, the print output is then likely to contain index offsets and other unwanted figures and notes that are outside the report frameworks. Reports can also be required individually, particularly when changes have been made and a reprint is required. The most flexible way of handling report output is to print each report separately, by defining its range and allowing it to be placed on a separate page. Figure 6.9 shows how this can be achieved most easily. The reports that are to be printed are given range names so that ranges can be easily entered, without reference to the spreadsheet cells. The name also tells the user what report it refers to. It can be a page reference of the report, or it can say what the report is, such as PROFIT or BSHEET.

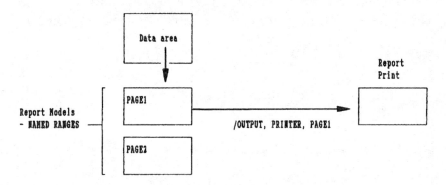

Figure 6.9   Report Selection

If a list of reports will also need to be printed, the output instructions can be preprogrammed in the form of a macro, which is a way of setting down the keyboard commands required as text, either on the spreadsheet or in a file. A macro program can be activated by calling up its name or its location on the spreadsheet. Using report range names not only makes it easier to build a macro but also makes it more understandable to the user.

ROUNDING ADJUSTMENTS

It is usually best to keep data in the smallest currency denomination possible, say £ or £'000, consistent with the size of the numbers. In this way the smaller numbers do not get lost. When it comes to reports they normally become more readable if the numbers are rounded up to, say, £'millions. This rounding up process can give problems of differences arising in totals that have been arrived at from different directions. There then needs to be some method built in to the reporting system that allows for such differences to be absorbed, so that totals that should agree do so.

Figure 6.10 shows the way in which this can be achieved. The basic problem is that when the detailed primary sales figures *A, B* and *C* are rounded into the report they total to £3.9m, whereas the rounded secondary data total comes to £3.8m. The rounded detail figures and their total are shown on the far right of the report. The rounding of the data total of 3824 is shown underneath it at line 21 (3.8). The difference between these two totals, -0.1 shown at line 33, must be taken off the detailed sales numbers in the report if the report total is to agree with the true rounded sales total at line 21.

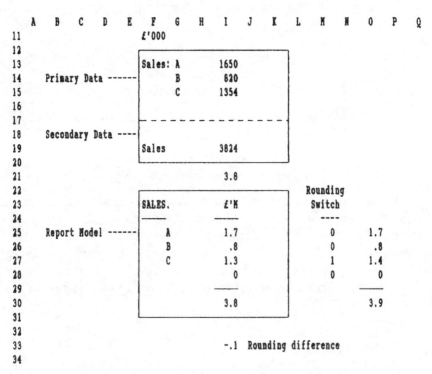

Figure 6.10   Report Rounding Adjustments

To adjust the report detail we have to define which line will take this adjustment. It can be the line that normally has the largest figure, or it can be a miscellaneous line, or any other that we care to choose. The way the line is selected is to have a rounding switch alongside the report lines concerned. When a switch is on (number 1) then that line takes the difference, when a switch is off (zero) it stays as it is. The switch operates, as we have seen before, as a coefficient or multiplier in the formula, adding in the difference if it is on. The formula that gives the sales of 1.7 against *A*, for example, is:

$$P25+J33*N25$$

A similar rounding difference can occur when a sales report, for example, includes the percentages of detailed sales figures to the total. These percentages might be rounded to integers or to one or two decimal places and it is unlikely that they would add up to 100 per cent. The percentage column would therefore also have to have a place defined to take any difference. This would be achieved by means of another set of switches, or maybe the same switches. It would certainly be unacceptable to have a report where percentages did not come to 100.

The only way to avoid rounding errors in reports, other than by the adjustment process described above, is to set up the dataset involved in rounded numbers in the first place. This is perfectly adequate where something like a budget or forecast is being re-ported, but it only shifts the rounding problem from one place to another if the forecasting model producing the numbers is working in a lower denomination. To make it work properly, the forecasting model has to produce its numbers in rounded values.

RUN CONTROL

Running a reporting system, from loading the first dataset to printing the last report, can require a complex sequence of commands at the keyboard. It not only demands a prolonged spell of concentration on the part of the operator, but any mistakes can completely invalidate the whole sequence and make it necessary to start again. There is also no guarantee that a mistake would be recognised if it was made.

The sequence of commands and decisions to be made for a typical report system, which is dealing with reports that have both separate reporting unit and consolidated figures on, is shown in Figure 6.11. Essentially it is going through two distinct stages. First, it loads each reporting unit dataset in sequence and runs the model each time, which gives those reports that have separate reporting unit numbers on. Second, it carries out a consolidation of all units and runs the model again to give reports with consolidated figures. The final stage is to print out the reports that have been produced.

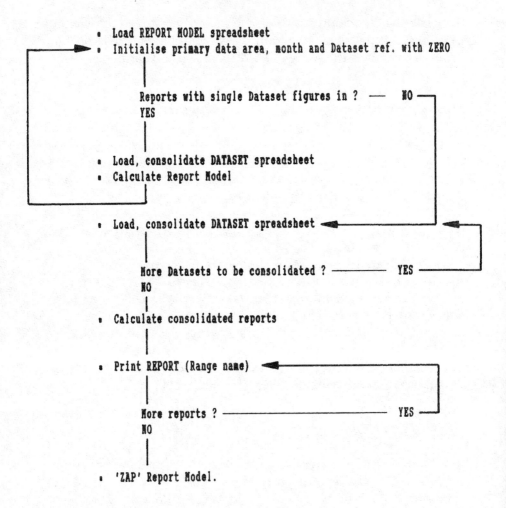

Figure 6.11   Run Control

There are two ways to control this type of system to try to avoid mistakes. The first is to list the sequence of commands at the keyboard by writing them down on an instruction sheet, then following those instructions each time reports are required. This still requires a period of concentration, with the possibility of part of the sequence being missed or incorrectly keyed in. However, it does avoid the need to rethink the command sequence each time a run is to be made.

The second way to control the system, and the one that ensures each run is the same, is to create a control program in the form of a macro, which can then be activated to run the system. This control program can be made up of separate macros that can be selected independently, perhaps by means of a menu. In this way different types of consolidation can be handled, as well as different report selections. The macro can also be written in the form of a computer program, as in Figure 6.11, so that decisions can be taken concerning the level of consolidation or the selection of reports required.

SUMMARY

□ A flexible and powerful reporting system can be produced by entering data required into separate spreadsheet datasets and loading or consolidating these into a report model.

□ Data are entered as positive numbers, unless otherwise defined. The way in which numbers are added or subtracted on a page is defined by the report model.

□ A dataset's reference number defines the company within the group, or site within the company. A set of row number references is used to identify data elements. Datasets also have a reporting period number, which is changed as required.

□ Annual budgets can be entered all together in months (or quarters) and indexed into the current month column by reference to the month number.

□ Forecasts can be reported by interfacing the report model dataset with the forecasting model.

□ Consolidations can be carried out quickly and reports can be produced that contain separate company as well as consolidated numbers. The key to this is the dataset reference number.

□ The report model calculates secondary or total numbers, which can then be used in reports and as controls.

□ The reports index data by reference to column and row offsets of that data, which are set up alongside the report pages. Reports can then be easily built and changed.

□ Rounding adjustments need to be defined if figures are to agree when they are supposed to.

□ Macros can be used to control the complex sequences of commands that run the system and print reports.

7

New Project Decisions

Whenever a business decides to develop a new product, take on a new contract, or expand by adding to its capacity, it has to work out whether or not the return from the project justifies the investment it will need to make. The size of this forecast future return will determine whether or not the project should go ahead. Some of the returns or benefits that could accrue from a project can be difficult to evaluate financially. The purpose of this chapter is, not only to show how the arithmetic can be done using models, but to show also how the appraisal of a project should be tackled.

INVESTMENT AND RETURNS

In Figure 7.1, three projects are shown, each of which require a significant investment and produce a good profit. A comparison of projects A and B shows that they both return a 40 per cent profit although the levels of investment required are different. The value of profits predicted is also different, with project B giving 30, against 20 for project A. If we had to decide, therefore, between project A or project B we might well go for project B, which gives more absolute profit, though we might have to convince ourselves that we could afford to invest the extra 25 in order to get this result. Profit expressed as a percentage, though, would appear to be an unreliable measure when making such comparisons, unless the amounts invested are about the same. If the investment in both A and B had been 50, then B would give a 60 per cent profit on the investment, which would then be a realistic measure of performance compared with project A.

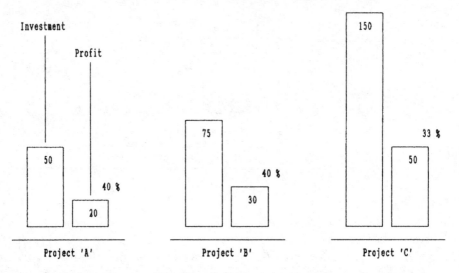

Figure 7.1   Investment and Returns

So the way to make more profit is usually to invest more. Constraints are put on this as in project C, where a very much larger investment is required and the business has difficulty, perhaps, in finding such an amount of cash. If it needed to be borrowed, the return might have to be even higher to give the added profit contribution. So it would not be just the size of the profit that determined whether or not we went ahead with a project, but also the size of the investment required. What is equally important is the timing of the investments and returns. If the returns did not materialise for several years, they would not be worth as much as those that were received sooner.

CASHFLOW TIMING AND VALUE

To look at these timing differences more closely, Figure 7.2 shows an investment of 100 which gradually earns compound interest at 10 per cent per annum until, by year 5, it is worth 161. So 161 is the future value of the investment. If this future value has its interest removed it becomes the value invested at the present time. So we can say that the value of the investment five years into the future, when discounted back to the present time at 10 per cent, gives a *Present Value* of 100. Clearly, therefore, the present value of future returns depends not only on how much they are expected to earn, but also how far into the future they are predicted to be.

Time elapsed : Years	0	1	2	3	4	5	Total
* Investment.	100						
* Future Value, with interest @ 10% p.a. compound.	100	110	121	133	146	161	
* Interest (Profit)	-	10	11	12	13	15	61
* Present Value of investment by Year 5 discounted to Year 0 @ 10% p.a.						100	
* Future Cashflows	(100) Outflow					161 Inflow	61
* Net Present Value of cashflow, discounted to Year 0 : — @ 10% p.a.	(100)					100	0
— @ 20% p.a. (Target)	(100)					65	(35)
* Future Cashflows	(100)			161			61
* NPV @ 20% p.a.	(100)			93			(7)

Figure 7.2 Cashflow Timing and Value

If we now think of this investment as a business project, you will see farther down in Figure 7.2 that a cash *Outflow* occurs when we invest 100 in the project and a cash *Inflow* occurs when the final return is received. The net cash inflow of 61 represents the final profit on the project. Below this you will see that these cashflows have been discounted back to *Present Values* at the interest rate of 10 per cent. The 100 invested is already at its present value and the 161 final return has a present value of 100 at that rate. The net present value of these future cashflows is therefore zero, which demonstrates that the discount rate that gives a net present value of zero, for a series of future cashflows, is the rate of return on the investment (10 per cent in this case).

This bank rate of interest, however, would not be sufficient to attract investors in our business, but they provide the biggest part of the capital. A new project would therefore need to earn more than bank rate to be a viable business proposition. But how much more? It rather depends on how risky a business we are in. The riskier the business, the higher interest premium an investor would expect. Studies in the USA, over a 65-year period from 1926 to 1991, have shown that the average risk premium for common stocks has been 8.5 per cent more than the return from Treasury Bills, which can be regarded as risk-free. In UK terms, therefore, a project that has the same level of risk as the market average of all stocks should be expected to give a return equal to Bank Rate plus an 8.5 per cent risk premium.

Individual industries can have risk factors that fall above or below this market average. The tendency of individual shares to move with the market as a whole is expressed as a covariance-based measure called the Beta Coefficient. The market as a whole has a Beta of 1. If the business is in property, air transport, or electronics, the Beta could be as high as 1.7. This could mean that the return required in these industries would be Bank Rate $+(1.7 \times 8.5)$ per cent, which would be 19.5 per cent with Bank Rate at 5 per cent per annum. Industries such as utilities and telecommunications, however, have a Beta of 0.8, so a project there could be expected to return about 12 per cent with a 5 per cent Bank Rate.

These rates of return required in different industries should be the target discount rates used to discount cashflows of particular projects. In Figure 7.2 the *Net Present Value* (NPV) of our project cashflows, discounted at the target 20 per cent, becomes a negative 35. This means that the project fails to meet the required return and could reduce the value of the business by 35 if we were to go ahead with it. Clearly therefore, any project that gives a positive NPV, at the target discount rate, should out-perform the market and add extra value to the business.

The effect of timing on cashflows can be seen at the bottom of Figure 7.2, where the final return now occurs in year 3, rather than year 5. The NPV of these cashflows at our target rate of 20 per cent is now just negative, at -7, which very nearly meets our requirements for the project to be approved. A change to the timing of the investment could also have a powerful effect on the NPV. If this project had its investment of 100 spread equally over the first two years, as well as having its returns in year 3, then the NPV would be zero and the project would achieve our target rate of return. Or, putting it another way, the internal rate of return of the project would be 20 per cent (our target).

PROJECT EVALUATION MODELS

Therefore, to evaluate a project, we will need to work out the cashflows and value those cashflows by calculating the NPV at our target discount rate. Figure 7.3 shows an overview of a model designed to produce such results. The structure of this model probably looks familiar by now. Most projects and new business proposals can be most easily evaluated by calculating receipts and payments directly from sales and costs in this way. This is because they are usually part of an existing business where cost structures and business interfaces are known. With green field and joint venture projects it can be different and I will cover these in this chapter.

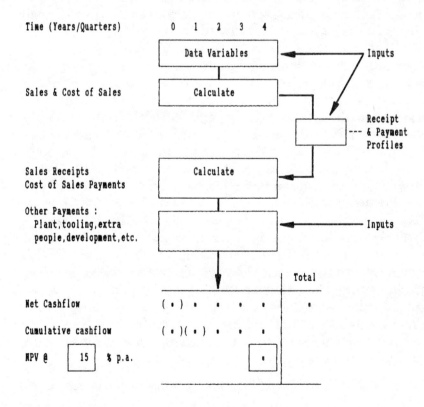

Figure 7.3   Project Evaluation Model: Structure

The timespan involved will depend on the type of appraisal being carried out. With a project such as the development of a new product, the forecast needs to look forward far enough to cover as much of the product life-cycle as possible; ideally the whole life-cycle. With a new business proposal we may only need to cover the contract to completion. The range of time to be covered will also determine whether the time periods used are years, quarters, or even months. The type of business being evaluated will also determine what data variables need to be set up and the level of detail to be built in. All projects and proposals are different from each other in some way and it is essential to approach evaluations with an open mind. It is almost impossible to build a general purpose model and not advisable to do so if each project is to be investigated thoroughly.

The investments required for the project are shown in Figure 7.3 in the section called *Other Payments*. These are shown as inputs, which they often are, but specific projects may be better handled by generating some of these payments by calculations from other data. Either way, the payments that have to be allowed for will need to be those that arise only if this project goes ahead. They must be incremental or additional payments to those that the business already incurs. The project evaluation is to be done so that a decision can be made whether or not to invest in the project. Anything that has been paid for in the past is not part of this decision. The decision will only be affected by future payments. There may also be times when the project being evaluated raises the possibility of, say, a factory extension at some time in the future. This should not be part of the present evaluation, but a separate decision, to be evaluated when the time comes.

The net cashflow calculated by the model is the basis for calculating the NPV; in Figure 7.3 the discount rate of 15 per cent has been set up as a variable. Our target return would be entered as the discount rate so that we could see whether or not the project was a good investment, by giving a positive NPV. This rate could also be changed to do several iterations until the NPV became zero, at which point we would know the internal rate of return of the project.

Spreadsheets have a function for internal rate of return, called IRR, which can be used as:

%pa=ROUND(IRR(Range of annual cashflows),No.of dec.places)

Internal rate of return calculations cannot always be relied upon, however, particularly if net cashflows go negative, then positive, then negative again. There can be more than one root to such equations. They can also go wrong if there is no investment or negative cashflow at the front end. For these reasons, I usually use the NPV function and change the rate to find the rate of return. Beware even here though, because the NPV function usually discounts the first year as well and therefore should be used as:

$$\text{Value} = \text{ROUND}(1\text{st year cash} + \text{NPV}(\text{Disc.}\%/100, \text{Range of other years}))$$

INCREMENTAL CASHFLOWS

There can be many influences on the resultant NPV of a project cashflow. Some are to do with value, some are to do with timing and some are to do with both value and timing. Figure 7.4 shows some of these incremental cashflow effects and the way they either reduce or increase the return on investment of the project. They very rarely all influence the case, but some of them do. To identify these effects on a specific project correctly is the most important part of the evaluation process.

Clearly, large early payments and small late receipts combine to give the lowest NPV for the project. Anything that can reduce the size of investments or cause them to be delayed can therefore improve the case. Terms of business that give rise to customer deposits well before delivery will also give more NPV. Other beneficial effects, shown at the bottom of the *Increased returns* stack in Figure 7.4, are *Grants* and *Tax savings*. Grants give extra cash in hand and can have a dramatic effect on the case, but no organisation or government body gives money for nothing and compliance with their requirements can often be too difficult or restrictive. I always get a bit nervous when tax savings are quoted as benefits, especially in long-term projects. There can be real tax advantages, but it pays not to make a case that depends on them for its success but, rather, treats them as additional benefits.

At the bottom of the list of those that reduce returns in Figure 7.4 you will see *Cannibalise other business*. The converse of this is shown on the increased returns side as *Spin-off in other business*. These are secondary effects that are often overlooked and difficult to evaluate, but which can have a significant effect on the business case. Other secondary effects shown are *Spare parts sales* and *Repair and maintenance* agreements. These are after-sales business that can go on for many years. When times are hard and prices of new business are low the prospect of such incremental business can significantly affect the case. In evaluating such projects we may need to look a long way ahead to decide whether or not they are feasible.

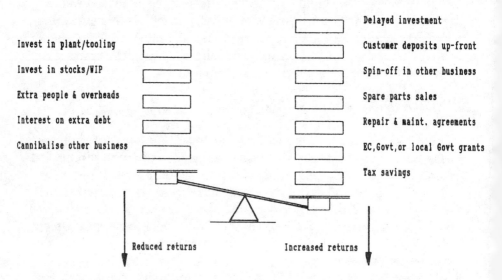

Figure 7.4   Incremental Cashflows

These secondary effects usually have some relationship to the core business of the project and can therefore be modelled, rather than simply input. If this can be achieved, then changes to the core business variables will automatically change the secondary cash-flows as well. This produces a properly integrated model that can react quickly and accurately to such changes. Spares sales, for example, invariably bear some relationship to original equipment in the field. This relationship will be based on service statistics, predicted reliability of the new product, manufacturing capability or cost and other factors. If no relationship can be found, then it is possible that the predicted secondary business might not be incremental to the project being evaluated and should be left out. Some extra business, such as maintenance agreements, could entail contractual negotiations with customers and might some-times be considered as separate decisions, to be evaluated inde-pendently.

JOINT VENTURE PROJECTS

Joint ventures have been singled out for special attention because it is easy to lose sight of what we are trying to do in evaluating such projects. Business collaborations are very common, particularly on larger projects. They enable resources and risks to be shared and can be the only means of getting new business, particularly in developing countries where local labour content is a primary concern. Joint venture projects can be complex, usually involving the sharing of work, technology, or marketing, and often leading to the setting up of separate companies or partnerships.

The evaluation of such ventures shown in overview in Figure 7.5, is a two-stage process. The joint project as a whole has to be evaluated first, to establish the total investment required and the returns to be generated. The profits from the venture then have to be shared between the partners so that they can calculate the returns they would get on their investments in the venture. Therefore, the business analyst's primary concern is the value of the return to the business he is working for, but to get that answer the joint venture project has to be evaluated first, which is the biggest part of the task.

Figure 7.5 also shows that the returns to the company investing in the joint venture are unlikely to be just a share of profits from the project. Added to this could be many other benefits. The manufacture or work that has gone into the joint venture (JV) projects could have been done in part, or even wholly, by the company and would be charged to the JV at an agreed price. The company might even supply plant, equipment, or tooling to the JV, or perhaps to the other partner if they were sharing production. All these sales to the JV, expressed in cash receipts terms, will add to the NPV of the company's net cashflow from the venture, after deducting the amount invested as equity capital.

As already stated, joint venture projects are usually complex and take shape after a protracted period of negotiation between the partners and ultimate customer. The structure of the model and the mechanisms for sharing work and profits are normally put together during these negotiations, so that they are in line with the contractual arrangements. Very often the model can be built and used to determine what the best methods or contractual arrangements might be. The company can look at different options and ways of optimising its return before sealing the contracts. In this way, the modelling approach becomes a very powerful tool in the process of understanding and agreeing how things should be done.

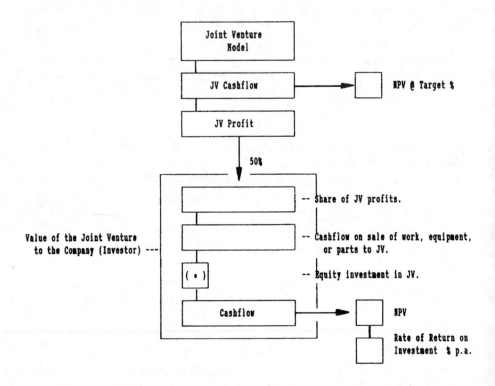

Figure 7.5 Returns from Joint Ventures

JOINT VENTURE MODEL STRUCTURE

Figure 7.6 shows the structure of a model for evaluating a joint venture project. The detailed variables and calculations required to derive the *Operating profit* would be peculiar to the project. The other modules would contain calculations that were more standardised and that could be used with other projects. Because of this, the operating profit module could be built as a separate spreadsheet and the results from this loaded or indexed into the more general model. The time taken to model and evaluate the project would then only be that required to build the operating profit section at the top.

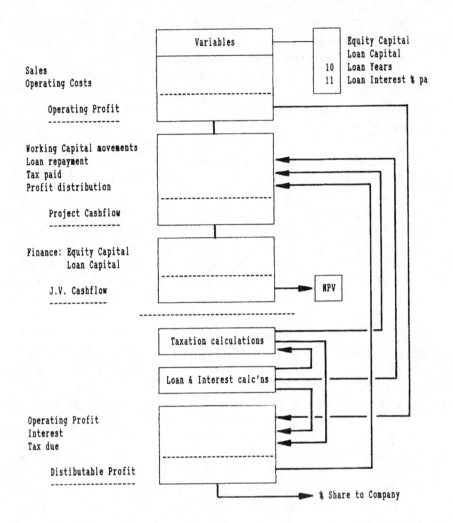

Figure 7.6 Joint Venture Model

The technique of loading one spreadsheet into another is covered in Chapter 6, dealing with report models. Using this technique for JVs, the project models could be separate spreadsheets, which are loaded as required into the top section of a standard JV model, which had been initialised to clear previous answers. A further development of this method could be the use of such a system to consolidate several projects to determine their overall effect on the business. A strategic plan, or just divisional plans, could also be built up in this way.

As joint venture projects are separate business ventures or

companies, profit figures are established so that tax can be calculated and net profits distributed. It is therefore easier to derive cashflow from profit via balance sheet movements in this type of model. You will see in Figure 7.6 that *Working Capital movements* only have been used to convert *Operating Profits*. If any incremental capital expenditure had been needed with this project the purchase payments related to this would have been included in the *Project Cashflow* section, with capital allowances being part of the *Taxation calculations*. If, on the other hand, fixed assets had been acquired with loan finance then payments related to them would be all or part of the *Loan repayments* shown in this section.

Profits are shown being distributed after tax. If the venture was an unincorporated partnership, however, the profits would be distributed before tax and the taxation calculations would be made separately for each partner. The taxation calculations in Figure 7.6 start with operating profits, deduct any allowances for capital expenditure and deduct loan interest, to give taxable profit. From this can be calculated not only the tax due, which reduces profit for distribution, but also tax to be paid, which reduces the project cashflow. The tax rules to be applied will, of course, depend on the country in which the venture is to be located. For operations overseas, a proper understanding of these rules will usually only be possible with the help of a local tax expert. At best it would be unwise, at worst it could be disastrous, for such advice to be ignored. There are all sorts of hazards to operating in other countries, but only adequate knowledge about them can help to make safe decisions about the project.

In Figure 7.6 the project cashflow will show the net outflow or funding requirements of the project. Below that is shown the way in which this is financed, both by *Equity Capital* from the joint venture partners and by any *Loan Capital*, or debt, required. Anyone wanting to understand the way that capital gearing works should build a model like this and play with it. Because interest is, in most countries, tax deductible, whereas dividends on equity capital are not, corporation tax will reduce the cost of debt capital compared with equity capital. There is another interesting relationship between debt and equity capital. If the return on the project is greater than the interest on debt, then using more debt increases the return on equity. Conversely, the return on equity is reduced if the rate of interest exceeds the return on the project. The use of more debt capital, however, increases the chances of the business running into difficulties and reduces its flexibility, because of the fixed future payments. The loan and interest calculations involved here can be handled most easily by using the functions provided with the spread-sheet.

CO-PRODUCTION VENTURES

Most ventures, where production is to be shared, come about either because work can be done more cheaply in the other country, or because that country's government wants a local share in production in return for purchasing your product. Often the company concerned retains the high technology part of the production operation and agrees to the overseas partner doing the rest. Sometimes, however, countries want to increase their technology base and this makes it necessary to transfer technology to them as well, as part of the agreement.

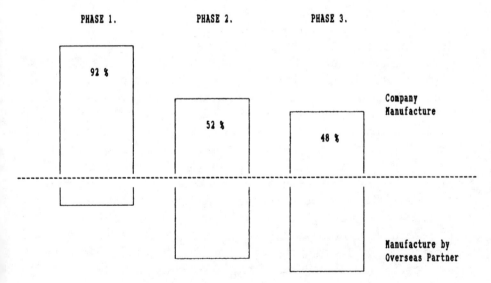

Figure 7.7   Co-production Joint Venture

The problems that can arise from sharing production are summed up in Figure 7.7. It does not usually happen all at once. Several phases may be involved during which the agreed content for local manufacture is progressively achieved. During this transitional period, the contractual agreement will need to be very clear about the way in which costs and revenues will be shared. In practice it will be difficult to understand what stage of this process has been reached. The share of revenues may, or may not, be based on the same shares as production.

In such a venture, the company could supply:

□ Kits of parts (more early, less later)
□ Raw materials (less early, more later)
□ Technology
□ Services (production engineering, sales, service, training)
□ Some tooling or plant.

The overseas producer might have to invest in:

□ Work-in-progress
□ Capital equipment and tooling
□ Additional factory space.

All these transactions will contribute to the respective partners' return on the project, in addition to their share of the profits. Pricing of such arrangements might be difficult to agree upon; a model that can help in the process of agreement is a very useful aid.

In overseas ventures of this sort, other things will also need to be allowed for in the model. The currencies involved will raise some problems. If the JV company is to operate overseas then the project evaluation will need to be prepared in the local currency, with sales to the JV and profits to the UK being converted at forecast exchange rates. Taxes, as stated in the previous section, will need to be calculated according to the rules of the country in which operations are to take place. There may be more than one type of tax to consider and, having established what profit could be distributed, it may also be difficult to repatriate that profit under the exchange regulations of the country concerned. Also, in evaluating an overseas project, we have to make allowances for difficult operating conditions. This can involve costs of overcoming a hostile climate, theft, bureaucracy, lack of local skills, poor transport and, sometimes, low quality standards of the production partner. Export credit arrangements would also have to be considered.

PRICING DECISIONS

Large contracts and many other types of business proposal frequently call for customer deposits and progress payments, as well as retentions of a final balance until some time after delivery. On the left side of Figure 7.8 is such a proposed contract where, for a price of 2550, we are predicting to get a deposit with order of 15 per cent and the balance of 85 per cent on delivery to site. You will also see that the monthly cash receipts have been discounted back to the present time at a monthly rate of 1.531 to give the NPV of 2362. The cell containing the answer 20 (per cent) is a formula that converts the input monthly rate into an annual equivalent. This monthly rate can therefore be changed until its annual value is our target. As we are only looking at receipts, the NPV can be used for comparison with other terms of business, but does not tell us much about the value of the proposed contract, unless we know the NPV of the payments also.

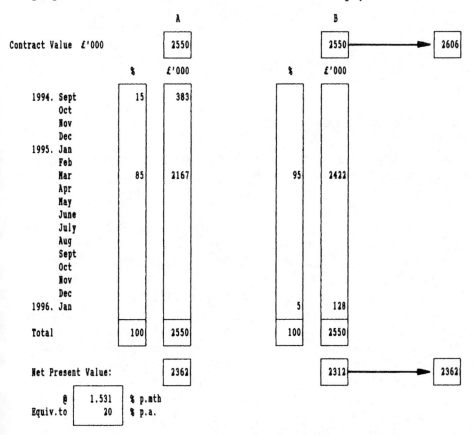

Figure 7.8   Pricing Decisions

On the right side of Figure 7.8 are the terms the customer has proposed. They are a lot less favourable than our own proposal, with no deposit and a 5 per cent retention ten months after delivery, by which time perhaps our equipment would have been commissioned. The NPV of the receipts under this arrangement would be 2312, some 50 less than we wanted. In order to get back to our original return we would have to propose to the customer that the price be increased to compensate for this loss. Using this model, the price in column B would be changed until the NPV at the bottom returned to 2362. This would then be the revised price quotation.

This type of model can be very useful in pricing different kinds of business proposal. It can also be used the other way round to propose improved terms of business that would compensate for a low price offer by the customer. It can be used, as well, to calculate the effect on NPV of changes in proposed delivery dates. This can be particularly useful when the contract involves multiple deliveries, within an overall contract price.

COMPARISON OF OPTIONS

Business managers are constantly looking at different ways of doing things, in order to see which might be the most cost-effective. If there is pressure on prices, or workload is dropping off, then cost reduction becomes the best means of survival for the business. Manufacturing processes will be compared, methods of production that avoid moving parts or work around will be evaluated and options of leasing rather than buying equipment will be checked. Some changes will be feasible, some will not, but subsequent changes in the economy or in technology might make it necessary to appraise such proposals again at some time in the future.

Figure 7.9 shows a comparison between the future payments (B) required to purchase a certain component for production and a proposal (A) to manufacture the same volume in-house. As you can see a model has been built to calculate the investment and costs of manufacture. It is obvious from the figures shown that to make the component in-house needs a big investment up front, but after an initial learning curve, the costs of manufacture become significantly less than those of purchase. The total cash payments up to year 4 are, in both cases, 3200 but the NPV of option B is significantly lower. This means that up to year 4 it would be less expensive to buy components (by 317 at present value).

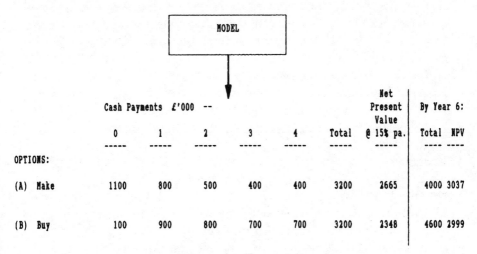

Figure 7.9   Comparison of Options

Taking a longer term view would show that the advantages of buying components would be gradually whittled away, until it finally became better to make them, although it would take several years. Even by year 6, there would not be a financial case for doing the job in-house. The decision whether or not to manufacture would therefore be very marginal and would depend on other factors as well. The example in Figure 7.9 assumes a clear-cut financial decision, but it would not be that clear in practice. The supplier of the bought-out components might offer some inducements to buy if he thought the business might disappear. Security of supply of these components might be a factor to be considered and making them might not be the solution to this problem. If the components were made in-house then there could be some spin-off in sales to other companies and this could influence the case. Then another major factor to consider would be the availability of the million pounds required to set up the in-house facility.

The problems placed in the way of making a decision in this case should have been part of the model that gives the answers to the manufacturing case. How much weight should be given to these risks and how they might affect our decision comprises the final section of this chapter.

RISK ANALYSIS

Any project evaluation assumes some level of confidence in the sales and cost figures. However, there will obviously be some risk of these not being attained and our decision about the feasibility of the project ought not to depend on a set of assumptions that might be too optimistic. To develop a view about the effect on the business case if things should not go that way, we need to calculate how the NPV of the cashflows might be affected by these risks. If the NPV remains positive, even after allowing for all the risks, then the project ought to be a good business proposition.

Figure 7.10 shows how this risk analysis is carried out. At the top are shown the risks to the venture, from 1 to 5. There could be a possibility that the project performs better than expected, but usually we are only concerned with the risk of things going wrong in such an analysis. In the boxes immediately below the risks are what we think might happen to our forecast assumptions if these risky events were to occur. This particular project, as you can see, depends on a gas turbine being engineered to produce more power. If that could be done then there would be an extended market for the more powerful machine. Failure to achieve that objective, or not achieving it in time, could therefore affect the sales expected. Poor engine reliability might mean higher warranty claims and manufacturing delays might mean penalties to be paid for late delivery.

How much these effects might influence the business case will depend on our view of the probability of them occurring. No future event is certain to occur, but equally no future event is without risk altogether. The assessment of probabilities is difficult and subjective. The only people who could assess the risks shown in Figure 7.10 would be the development and production engineers involved with the project. Their assessments might also be influenced by previous experience. When these probabilities have been decided, then they can be set up into a *decision tree*, as in Figure 7.10. The top of this tree ends in the single twigs, or *nodes* as they are called, shown in the column for Risk 5. The top line of these probabilities then reflects the risk of everything going wrong and the bottom line the risk of nothing going wrong. The lines in between contain every possible combination of those risks.

The probability at each node is shown on the right in the *Prob.%* column and is derived by multiplying all the percentage probabilities on that line. The project model is then primed with the effects of the risks either in or out, according to whether the probability line says yes or no. The top node, for example, which gives an NPV answer from the model of -578, would have included all the effects in the model run. The NPV of the decision node is then the product of the probability percentage and the NPV from the model run. It is this column, on the far right in Figure 7.10, that is added up when all the model runs are complete to give the NPV of the project, after allowing for all risks.

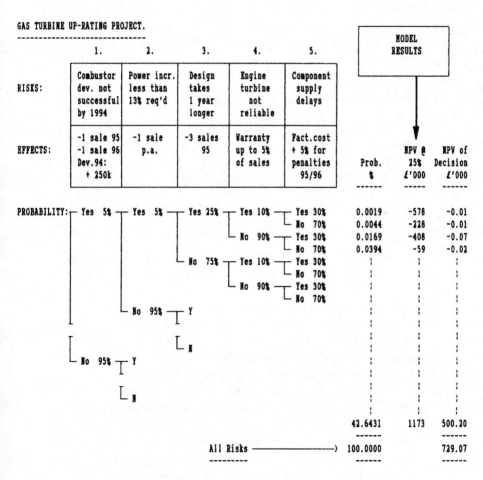

Figure 7.10   Risk Analysis

The probability percentage column totals to 100, which demonstrates that the decision tree percentages have been set up properly. The NPV of the model results for the bottom node line shows 1173. This would have been the result from the model before any risk assessment had been made, or without any risks being involved. The extent to which this has changed to 729.07 represents the effect of risk on the project. The method of getting this answer is clearly not an exact science, because the probabilities and even the risks and effects involved can only be estimated. The future is uncertain, but we can only guess at how uncertain. Some assessment of risk is usually worth making, especially with projects that have NPVs close to zero. What is certain is that using a model is essential to this type of analysis.

SUMMARY

- An investment appraisal has to take into account not only the profit to be made, but also the size of the investment required.
- The effect of cashflow timing on project value can be measured by discounting periodic cashflows back to present values. The discount rate to be used should be Bank Rate plus a risk premium of 8.5 per cent multiplied by the industry Beta Coefficient.
- A project appraisal model is best if tailor-made for the job. It will normally convert sales and costs to cashflow via capital employed movements.
- Only incremental payments and receipts should be included in the evaluation and all possible influences on the project should be considered.
- In joint ventures the total project has to be evaluated first, then the returns to the partners can be established.
- JV models, designed specifically for each project, can interface with more standardised modules for calculating loan and interest payments, taxation and distributable profit.
- Tax deductible interest makes debt capital cheaper than equity. Return on equity is increased if the project rate of return is greater than the debt interest rate.
- Overseas co-production can require quite complex models, particularly if production changes are to be phased in. There can be many hazards to be allowed for in costs.

□ Pricing models use NPV to trade-off price against cashflow timing.

□ Manufacturing options can be compared by reference to their NPVs, but the forecast must look forward far enough to detect shifts in economic viability.

□ An analysis of risks is usually worthwhile, particularly if the original project appraisal gives a low or near-to-target rate of return.

8

Model Design and Construction

I hope that by now you have become interested enough in the ideas and techniques in the previous chapters to want to model your own business. This can be done by going straight to the keyboard and constructing the program as you go along. I have seen it done this way and I wouldn't recommend it. A lot of preparation and thinking has to take place first if a model is to be designed so that it accurately reflects the business operation and can be used effectively. Any good design is usually both functionally efficient and a thing of beauty. A neat and elegant computer program is no exception to this. If a model is built in an organised and logical way and is laid out so that you can see what you are trying to do, then it is more likely to be efficient. The design process itself makes you analyse the business more thoroughly, so that the eventual model should behave as expected.

THE DESIGN AND BUILD PROCESS

Figure 8.1 shows the way I design and build models. It is a way of working that suits me, but is also more likely to produce a model that is right first time. The early processes, shown at *1* and *2* in this diagram, are concerned with putting thoughts on paper. An overview is constructed first, which shows how the model is to work and what answers we want. Then a more detailed layout of the proposed spreadsheet is drawn, which becomes the blueprint from which the model is built on the computer screen. These parts of the build process are the ones that produce dividends later on.

As you can see from Figure 8.1, the framework of the spreadsheet is constructed (at *3*) by putting in the line narrative and column headings. At this stage any additions or changes can be easily made should something have been forgotten. When the outline of the total spreadsheet has been prepared in this way, a print is produced with its column and row borders and used to construct the calculation formulae (at 4). This is the best way to set up formulae. It is almost impossible to do it directly onto the spreadsheet because the screen does not show enough to see quickly the cell references you need. I usually write in only the key formula that is to go in the cell at the first column and row of that particular calculation. The replication of this is then done on screen when the key formula has been entered (5).

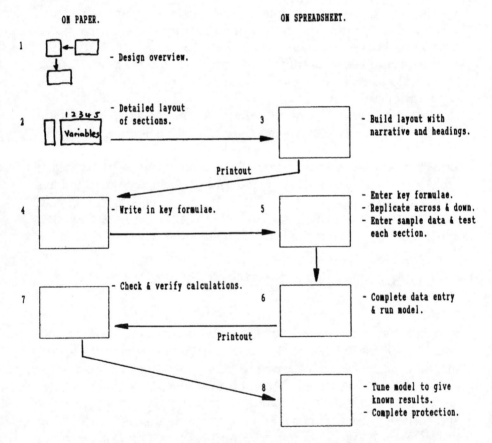

Figure 8.1   Model Design and Build

As each section or module of the spreadsheet is constructed on screen, sample data is also entered so that the calculations can be tested progressively. In this way there should be no need to check backwards if errors in later sections show up. When the model has been fully built, the rest of the data is entered and a full run of the model is done. Sometimes several runs are required so that switches and other selectors can be tested. It is important at this stage not to take any calculation for granted, but to test every possible combination of variables. The final process, before using the model in anger, is to tune it, using actual or other data that will give known results.

THE DESIGN OVERVIEW

The design overview is shown in Figure 8.2. This is where the design concepts of the model are thought out and the scope and logical progression of the model are clearly defined. This particular model, CYCLE1, is used in the last chapter of this book to demonstrate the use of models in business decision making. There you will see the actual spreadsheet construction. The design overview here shows how it all started.

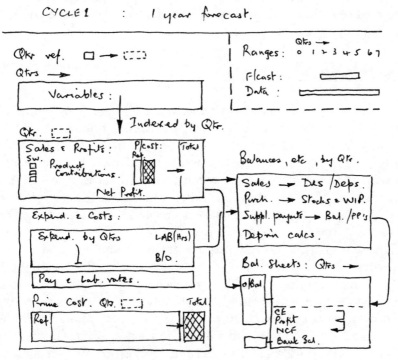

Figure 8.2 Design Overview

You can see from Figure 8.2 that the design is really a set of notes, or reminders, of how the model will work. It also shows the major information flows, which may well influence the eventual layout. There is no attempt made at this stage to design the spreadsheet layout. We simply want to define the content. You can see that it has been decided that the model will work in quarters and that only one year will be reported, making it necessary to have a range of data that spans six months either side of this. You can also see that the model is to run one quarter at a time. The indexing of variables in this way implies the eventual use of named ranges. The construction of balances and reports by overlaying quarterly calculations is defined very simply, without any detail about the use of matrices.

The *Expenditure and Costs module* will be a more complex section. Labour and purchases have to be constructed with quarterly slices and pay rates generated for each quarter from the labour hours. These costs are then to be related to the outputs for each quarter to produce a prime cost of sales total. This is the source of prime cost in the *Profits module,* so both are shown as cross-hatched areas to remind me to index it in this way, using the product references. The variables required have not yet been defined. This will be the next stage in the model design process.

THE DEFINITION OF VARIABLES

Most variables are specific to a particular business. Those shown in Figure 8.3 are the result of an investigation of how a cycle frame building business would operate. Most of them are also needed because of the way we want the model to calculate certain results. As with the overview, we are again trying to decide the variables required and the form they will take, rather than the layout of the spreadsheet. Once again, the chart is simply a set of notes which can be used to construct the data tables required.

This part of the design process is important because, if any variables are forgotten or not properly constructed, it might be difficult to build them into the spreadsheet model after the others have been set up. This could be especially so if named ranges have been used, or if the layout has been arrived at to make data input logical and easy. As you will see in the next chapter, this is what happened with the CYCLE1 model and I ended up having to squeeze data tables into the model in some odd places.

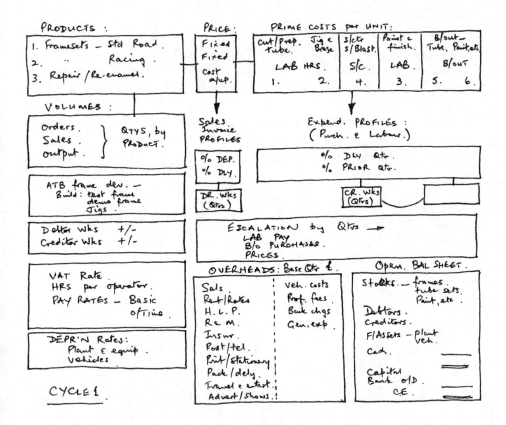

Figure 8.3 Definition of Variables

This chart shows not only the range of variables, but also the way in which data tables will be analysed. Also shown, in some cases, are the ways in which data will be entered, such as whether it will be at base-quarter levels, or whether it will be entered only in the base quarter and any increases or decreases to that shown separately. We will look at different data input methods in a later section, but at this design stage all these possibilities need to be thought out clearly. Pricing, for example, partly at fixed levels and partly by cost mark-up, will make it necessary to build in some form of switch that will tell the model which of these it is looking at. It is sufficient in the design, though, simply to define the requirement for different pricing methods.

SPREADSHEET LAYOUT

Having defined how the model will work and the type and structure of variables to be used, we then have to decide how all this can best be built into a spreadsheet. You will see from Figure 8.4 that I am once again using CYCLE1 as an example, though this model is perhaps not too typical in terms of spreadsheet layout. It was designed to be compact, but it still serves the purpose of showing how to do the layout of a model.

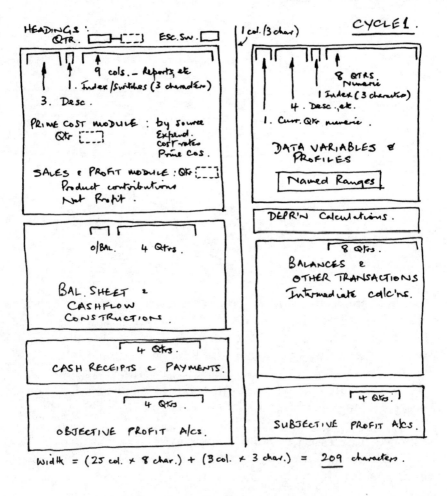

Figure 8.4 Spreadsheet Layout

The main considerations will be to keep the main inputs and compatible calculation groupings within separate areas, as well as to organise the columns so that the model can be printed across a page of computer paper. As far as the latter consideration is concerned, I normally print out in condensed form so that the page can comfortably accommodate up to 25 columns of 9 characters, or 225 characters overall. Getting more columns in means reducing their width. Some columns, as you can see in Figure 8.4, are no more than three characters wide, which is sufficient to take switches and vertical lines. General columns have also been reduced down to eight characters each, so that the total character count fits the page.

This stage of design is really the blueprint from which the spreadsheet will be built and it often pays to do the layout in even more detail depending on the complexity of the model, though a large number of products or customers should not be confused with complexity.

BUILDING THE SPREADSHEET FORMULAE

Once the spreadsheet text framework has been set up and printed off, the calculation formulae can be constructed. The cell in the first column of a row of calculations, or the top left cell of a block, is usually the key formula to be written on the printout. It is easier to write a formula on in this way because all the cell references required can be seen on the page. Once these key formulae have been established and then entered on to the spreadsheet, they can be replicated into the other columns of the row or block.

The replication, or copying, of a formula across and down a spreadsheet requires concentration. You have to think whether or not each variable is to be constant across the row or down the column or both, or whether they can be automatically changed to new column or row references. The normal way to handle these different needs is to define the constants across the page by putting a $ sign in front of the column reference of the variable, or defining the constants down the page by putting a $ in front of the row reference. I find that the resultant formula becomes very difficult to read using this method. I prefer to use the facility in SuperCalc, which allows you to use relative references in all formulae, but to hold variables constant by using the adjustment option when replicating.

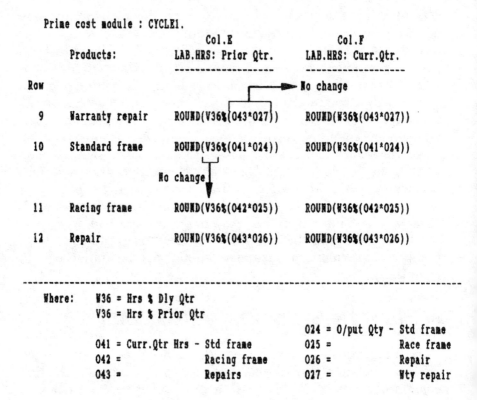

Figure 8.5   Replication of Formulae

In Figure 8.5 you can see how this can be thought out beforehand. The key formula at E9 is to be copied to F9 and I have marked above O43 and O27 in that formula to indicate that these variables will remain constant. Similarly, the key formula at E10 has been marked underneath to indicate that V36 will remain constant when copying downwards. This facility is flexible, easy to use and if you make a mistake the replication can be done again very quickly without the need to change the formula by altering absolute references. Incidentally, I've made problems for myself in the replication of the formulae in Figure 8.5 by putting warranty repair at Row 9, rather than in the same order as the output quantity table, where it is shown at the bottom. The same sort of problem can arise if the data table, or even the calculation matrix, is not continuous and uniform both across and down.

MODULAR DESIGNS

We have looked at ways of building models as separate sections or modules: in Chapter 6 with report models and in Chapter 7 with projects and joint ventures. There are really two ways of building and using such models and these are shown in Figure 8.6. The first method is to build separate calculation modules within the same spreadsheet. With this method, figures from one module are indexed into another and back again, sometimes under the control of switches. In this way, sets of calculations can be performed to give specific results, but switched out if not required. The modules can be built and tested separately and a complex model constructed more easily.

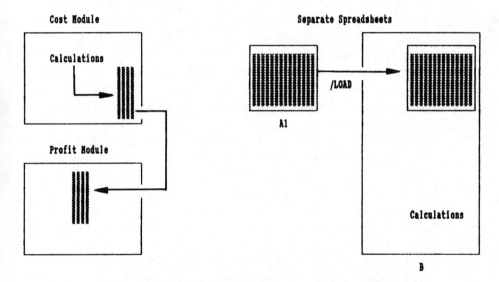

Figure 8.6 Modular Designs

The second method is an extension of the first, but the data and basic calculations for a particular project are set up on a separate spreadsheet and then loaded into a host model. This model will be built of separate modules and designed to give a selection of reports. You will recall that this loading process will usually transfer values only, so that formulae don't suddenly find themselves in an environment where their references are alien to their new location. This method gives a flexibility to a model, which enables consolidations to be done and allows for the effects of project combinations to be tested.

The use of macros as control programs with such models also enables them to be run more effectively by reducing the risk of command errors.

USING THE COMPUTER SCREEN

What you see on a computer screen is usually only a small part of a spreadsheet. It helps, when building a model, if it is structured so that only a minimum movement of this window is necessary to make changes or run the model. Some of the factors that need to be considered are:

☐ The home window, or the top left corner of the spreadsheet, should contain as many of the key switches and results as possible. The results will include such things as the NPV of a project, or the cashflows and profits over several years. The year or quarter selector would also be included within this area so that different periods could be run and the results seen as well.

☐ Where there are other key answers that result from switch changes, then it pays to have the switch alongside the answer, so that you don't have to move the window to see the result after changing the switch.

☐ It helps to have data located in a common area, so that inputs and changes can be made with the least movement about the spreadsheet.

☐ The use of titles on the spreadsheet makes it easier to enter data into the correct column and row. This is the facility that allows you to keep the column and row headings on the screen as you move about the spreadsheet.

☐ Other things to be included in the headings of the spreadsheet in the home window are cell references of spreadsheet macros and the print ranges for parts of the spreadsheet. In the latter case it helps to have in front of you the ranges of reports or prints that are used regularly.

☐ If all the key results cannot be kept within the home window, then they should be contained within a window that can be reached by paging down, so that you can view them and then return quickly to the switches or selectors.

All these factors are unlikely to be allowed for in any model, but the principles involved should be borne in mind whenever a spreadsheet is being built, so that it becomes as easy to use as possible.

DATA INPUT METHODS

The accuracy with which data is entered and changed will determine the integrity of the results from the model. Even though the model's calculations have been thoroughly checked, putting an element of data in the wrong time period can completely invalidate the answers. In the worst case you might never know it was wrong. The basic method of avoiding this is shown in Figure 8.7 where, as stated earlier, a spreadsheet printout is used as an input document. Then, after entries have been made, this document is checked against another printout that includes those entries. If these agree then it is all down to writing data onto the printout correctly in the first place. At least these manual changes can be seen and, if the input sheets are retained, a record will be available of what has been done.

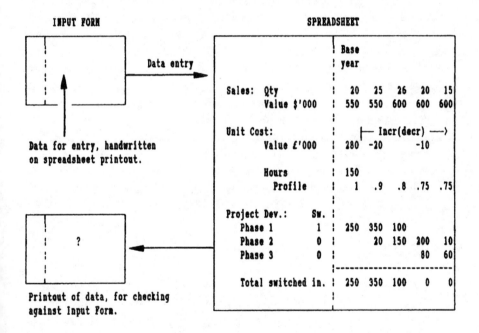

Figure 8.7   Data Input Methods

Shown also in Figure 8.7 are different ways of entering data on the spreadsheet. In each case, of course, the model's calculations are designed to work with that particular data format. The format shown for the sales numbers is straightforward, but the narrative must clearly define what the data purports to be, in this case values in thousands of dollars. In this format, values can be at base-year levels, or perhaps at escalated levels. Base-year values will show step changes that are unmasked by inflation movements.

The next two methods, shown under unit cost in Figure 8.7, allow for a single entry of value or hours in the base year, with entries in later years only if there is a change predicted from that level. In the case of the cost value, only increases or decreases in value are recorded. The hours are defined by means of a profile or coefficient, which would be multiplied by the base-year hours to give the level in each year. The profile shown would represent either a learning curve for a new product, or perhaps a planned cost saving programme. Both of these methods make for economy of entry and speed of change. They also provide an easy means of carrying out 'what happens if?' analyses.

The last method shown relates to a development project where there are various options. It may be that each phase of the development gives an increased sales prospect for the product, or even opens up new markets. Putting in switches against each of these phases enables them to be switched in or out of the total at the bottom. This total, when incorporated in the model proper, makes it possible to run the model with different levels of development included so that all options are evaluated. The advantages of this method are that the detailed development costings can be held as data and that 'what happens if?' runs can be made without having to take out or change any of those data, with all the potential for error that this would entail. The formula in the total line would be the sum of the products of switch and value on each line.

CHECKS TO AVOID ERRORS

Computers are arithmetically accurate and computer printouts tend to be regarded as authentic because of that. What is often forgotten is that the computer only does what the program tells it to do. When schedules and pages of figures had to be handwritten, accountants devised a technique for checking additions, called cross-casting. This process entailed adding numbers across as well as down the page so that, if the total of all the columns equalled the total of all the rows, you could be sure of the accuracy of any total (unless there were compensating errors). With the advent of spreadsheets it became possible for anyone to build up a page of figures and get the program to add them down, simply by defining the range of rows to be included. The totals across the rows could also be added and that column could be added down as well to give a total for the whole page. If the computer was doing the arithmetic there should not be any worries. However, if a new row was inserted at the bottom and the SUM formulae had not been changed, then the bottom line totals would no longer be correct.

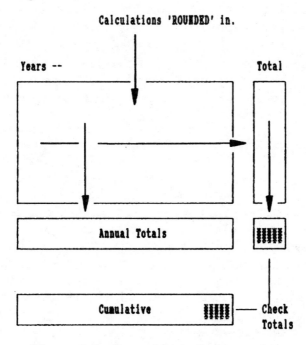

Figure 8.8   Spreadsheet Cross-casting

Figure 8.8 shows how such problems can be avoided by reverting to the old principle of cross-casting. In the spreadsheet shown, the sum of the *Annual Totals* has been arrived at by calculating cumulatives, as would be done for a cashflow statement or project appraisal, for example. This cross-check total could equally well have been shown separately within a single cell. The important point of this is that the grand total down should be situated near to the grand total across, so that a visual comparison can be made. Such methods can be employed where any matrix of numbers is to be added. Another reminder, shown in Figure 8.8, is to round numbers into the matrix rather than formatting them, so that all numbers on the page are what they appear to be.

PRINTING

Designing reports that can be printed out on an acceptable size of paper is an integral part of the model building process. Most forecasting model reports will have a number of columns, representing years or quarters. Accommodating this width usually means using a condensed print format. The range references of the individual reports, or groups of reports, can be included within the headings area of the model, so that they can be seen in the home window when selecting prints. Another method, which makes selection easier, is to make each report a named range and to select print output by using the name, rather than the range references. A sequence of reports can be printed in this way by building the commands into a macro.

TESTING

The testing process should start while the model is being built. Sample data should be entered into sections as formulae are being constructed. In this way the calculations can be proved as you go along, particularly if sections are self-contained. Such checks can usually only be made by manually repeating the arithmetic, but visual checks can sometimes also be built in to show whether things are correct or not. Typical of these checks are cross-casting and totalling of percentages to 100. Another check is to get to the same answer from different directions. Examples of this would be different analyses of sales, or both objective and subjective profit accounts.

When a forecasting model has been built, all remaining data should be entered and further checks should be concentrated on either the first or an early time period where the results are known. We looked at this in some detail in Chapter 3 by going through the model tuning sequence. Either actual or, perhaps, budget data should be used in this process.

With a project appraisal model, we don't usually have the luxury of knowing what the answer should be, even at the front-end. Apart from the earlier arithmetical checking, we have to ensure that the data we are using is cross-checked, if at all possible, with some other source. Another useful approach is to do some very basic 'back of a cigarette packet' calculations relating to the project, to see if these answers are something like those the model predicts. It is surprising how revealing such crude arithmetic can be.

SUMMARY

☐ Time spent designing a model pays dividends later.

☐ The initial design overview is a way of putting thoughts onto paper about how the model will work. Part of this process is to map out the variables required and the form they will take.

☐ The spreadsheet layout defines in more detail how the model will be constructed and forms the blueprint from which it will be built on the computer.

☐ Key formulae are constructed on a print of the spreadsheet framework; they are then entered and replicated on the computer.

☐ Modular designs help in the building process, make models more flexible and enable parts to be standardised.

☐ Designing a model to use the computer screen effectively helps in reducing data entry and run times.

☐ Several different methods of organising data can be employed, so that changes are kept to a minimum and 'what happens if?' analyses can be more easily carried out.

☐ Disciplines of cross-casting and other checks should be employed on a spreadsheet to ensure its integrity.

☐ Reports should be designed to fit the printed page and to be easily selected.

☐ Testing must be thorough and complete if the business analyst is to stake his reputation on the results.

9

Using Models for Business Decisions

INTRODUCTION

Having looked at ways of building models in previous chapters, I now want to explore the ways in which financial models can be used as aids in the process of making business decisions. To do this I have built two models of a cycle frame-building business and primed them with realistic yet hypothetical variables. These models are then used to show the effects of different actions and to investigate ways of optimising performance. The choice of this type of business is due, in part to my previous experience of such an operation, but mainly because it possesses many of the complexities of a much larger business while being small enough to use for illustration.

The chapter is in three parts. Part A gives some background information on cycle frame building to show how this is done in a small business of this kind. I have also shown the business interfaces, both internally and externally. Together, these two overviews will help to explain why the models are constructed as they are.

Part B shows how a short-term forecasting model of the business, CYCLE1, has been built and how the various calculations are derived. The model data are set up in such a way that the forecast shows a serious cashflow problem. The later sections of this part look at how this position might be improved and what the model predicts would be the outcome. Finally, there are some conclusions about likely courses of action.

Part C uses a second model, CYCLE2, which has been built specifically to decide whether or not to buy and use shotblasting plant in-house, rather than continuing to put this work out to a sub-contractor. This model is explained and possible flaws in the base case are examined before running the model to see what effect such weaknesses might have on the case. Conclusions are then drawn about the business case for going ahead with this investment.

PART A: THE FRAME BUILDING BUSINESS

Frame building

A handbuilt cycle frame, which this sort of business produces, is constructed from lightweight, very strong steel tubing. The lengths of tubing that form the rigid frame are held together by brazed joints, where low melting point bronze or silver rods are melted with a flux to flow into the joint, which is heated with an oxyacetylene flame. The exotic alloys and the thin walls of the tubing make this a very skilled job. The tubing can easily be damaged and lose its tensile strength if heat is applied in the wrong way.

In most handbuilt frames, lugs are used to hold the tubing together while brazing takes place. They also help in the process of brazing, where the small gap between the tube and the lug helps the brazing metal flow into the joint by capillary action. If the brazing process has been skilfully done, the joints on the finished frame take very little cleaning up afterwards. Some frame-builders cut away the lugs into distinctive decorative patterns before using them, to make the frame look more attractive.

The lengths of the tubes and the angles at their joints determine the size and riding position of the user, as well as the responsiveness and feel of the cycle. Different configurations are used for different types of cycle. A touring frame needs comfortable steering with plenty of trail, and good wheel clearance so that mudguards can be fitted. A racing frame needs more acute angles to throw the weight forward and make it more responsive. Wheel clearance can be small, making the frame smaller and lighter and the wheelbase shorter. A mountain bike frame needs greater strength, particularly at the front, with more ground clearance at the pedals, so that downhill impacts and muddy conditions can be handled. These bikes also have thumb selectors for gear changes so that the rider can hold the bars at all times, as well as having a much different riding position.

To get the required frame size and shape, tubes, which are bought as a set, have to be cut and mitred accurately. The mitres at the ends form the joints, where one tube wraps round another at the correct angle. The accuracy of this fit determines the way in which the braze joins the tubes and gives the joint its strength. The joint ends and lugs also have to be thoroughly cleaned before brazing.

Figure 9.1 shows the sequence in which joints are brazed. To build the frame in this way, most builders now use a jig with tube clamps that set the joint at the required angle. These clamps incorporate heat sink blocks of aluminium, to dissipate the heat around the joint and cool it more quickly. This way the next joint can be brazed without producing stresses in the frame that is clamped in the jig. You will see from Figure 9.1 that the front triangle (*joints 1–4*) is built first. The rear dropouts are then brazed into the two chain stays before these are joined to the bottom bracket. The seat stays complete the main frame, with a final joint on the outside of the seat lug. Both the chain stays and seat stays will be strengthened and serve as mountings for brakes and mudguards by brazing on bridges, which join each pair of stays near to the seat tube ends. Forks are built up separately and, finally, fittings such as cable guides and water bottle mountings are brazed on.

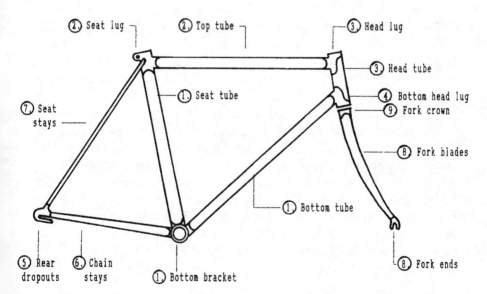

Figure 9.1   Cycle Frame and Build Sequence

Finishing off the frame entails first a shotblasting process that cleans and smooths the surface. Next the frame is sprayed with enamel in a spraybooth. Several coats are applied, each one in turn being allowed to dry. The enamelled frame is then baked in an oven, before finally having its transfers applied.

Business interfaces

The interfaces with the frame-building business will determine the way in which the model is constructed. Figure 9.2 is a diagrammatic representation of the supply of materials, equipment and labour, as well as the processes that build the frames and finally despatch them to customers. Outside suppliers provide the tubing, lugs and consumables, all of which give rise to stocks subsequently used in production. Suppliers also provide the heat, light, power and other overheads of the business. Wages and salaries are, of course, not bought on credit, but paid for in cash as they are earned. There are also outside suppliers of new plant, equipment and motor vehicles that are planned for the business. The development of a new mountain bike frame has been assumed to be done outside the business and is therefore also a purchased service.

The building processes follow the practices discussed in the previous section, with the tube being cut and mitred, brazed and finally painted. At each stage the materials required are drawn from stocks. Prior to painting, frames are delivered to and collected from the shotblasting sub-contractor. In Part C we will evaluate a proposal to do this shotblasting within the company.

The completed new frames might be held for a while as finished stock before being delivered to shops and some private buyers who build them up into complete cycles. Frames coming in for repair are usually those that are to be re-enamelled, necessitating an initial visit to the shotblasters. There may be, however, some repairs to be done under warranty, free of charge. Frames held in the factory during repair are, of course, still the property of the customers, so they never appear in finished stocks, though the value of work done can be part of work-in-progress.

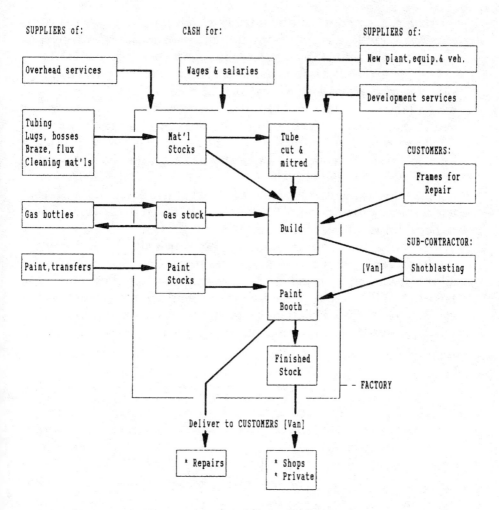

Figure 9.2 Cycle Business Interfaces

PART B: THE SHORT-TERM FORECASTING MODEL CYCLE1

Model structure

Figure 9.3 shows the structure of the model CYCLE1, which is designed to forecast one year ahead. It is built to work in quarters rather than months, mainly because forecasting to months is unreliable and rarely worthwhile. The *Base Data* and *Intermediate calculations* are located on the right-hand side of the spreadsheet, with most of the final calculations and reports being on the left.

This structure allows for a more compact model, with data alongside the model calculations that use it. It also allows for a short model (some 174 lines in total), which makes for easier data input and change. Such a structure has a disadvantage during the model building process, in that reshaping one side, by inserting or deleting lines for example, automatically reshapes the other side. This can be difficult to handle if building is at an advanced stage and several named ranges are involved. However, once constructed, it is easy to use and quick to print out. However, initial design of the layout has to be an important part of the building process.

The model runs one quarter at a time, which allows for detailed quarterly costs, sales and profit figures to be seen. Having to hold all this information for all quarters would make the model far too large to handle. Data are organised within named ranges so that they can be indexed in calculations by reference to the quarter number. Balance sheets, cashflow and profit reports are built up as each quarter is run.

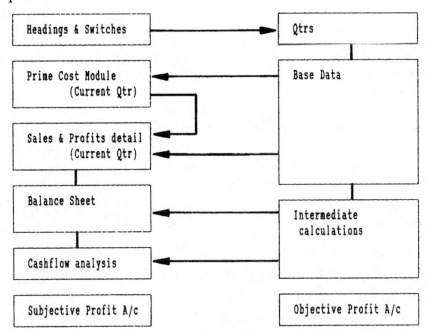

Figure 9.3   Short-term Forecasting Model: Structure

Base data

Figures 9.4, 5 and 6 show the base data section of the model. The boxes enclose the data that can be input or changed. At the top of Figure 9.4 is the named range *QTR*, which contains the quarter references. Above this are the *column offsets*, which are used to run the model and index those quarterly data columns. Most other data tables below also have range names so that they can be indexed in this way. Down the left side of the base data area is a column that indexes the data variable for the currently defined quarter. This simplifies calculation formulae that can reference this column, rather than having to keep indexing the data tables. Immediately to the left of the data tables are the *row offsets* of the named ranges. Indexing data through this column for the row offsets makes it easier to replicate formulae downwards when building the model.

Curr.Qtr					0	1	2	3	4	5	6	7
1/94	Quarters	QTR	0		3/93	4/93	1/94	2/94	3/94	4/94	1/95	2/95
1.005	Escalation: Lab.pay	ESC	0		.995	1	1.005	1.01	1.0151	1.0202	1.0253	1.0304
1.0075	S/ctr		1		.9926	1	1.0075	1.0151	1.0227	1.0303	1.0381	1.0459
1.0075	Mat'ls		2		.9926	1	1.0075	1.0151	1.0227	1.0303	1.0381	1.0459
1	Prices		3		1	1	1	1	1	1	1	1
3	Sales order lead: Qtrs [1]											
	VAT rate: % [17.5]			85	% of total purchases.							
	Programme Qtys:											
200	Orders: Standard	ORDER	0		130	150	200	150	120	150	150	150
70	Racing		1		30	40	70	60	60	75	100	100
0			2									
100	Sales: Standard	SALES	0		120	100	100	180	120	100	100	180
30	Racing		1		24	20	30	60	70	50	55	96
30	Repairs		2		50	40	30	60	55	45	35	60
140	Output: Standard	OPUT	0		120	100	140	140	120	100	100	180
30	Racing		1		24	20	30	60	70	50	55	96
30	Repair		2		50	40	30	60	55	45	35	60
2	Wty repair	WTY	0		1	2	2	2	2	1	2	1
	Prices:		M/u Sw									
195	Standard	PRICE	0	0	195	195	195	195	195	195	200	200
295	Racing		0	1	295	295	295	295	295	295	310	310
1.67	Repairs		1	2	1.67	1.67	1.67	1.67	1.67	1.67	1.67	1.67

Figure 9.4   CYCLE1 Base Data: Periods, Escalations, Programmes and Prices

Figure 9.4 has some further points of interest. The base quarter is Qtr.1 (Qtr.4/93), as is seen from the escalation coefficients being 1. All financial values in these data tables, including those in Figures 9.5 and 6, are set at this base-quarter level and escalated accordingly when the model is run. The *Programme Quantity* tables allow for *Orders, Sales* and *Outputs* to be separately defined. Order programmes are required to calculate customer deposits with order and, towards the top of Figure 9.4, is a variable (*Sales order lead*) that defines how long before sale the average order is taken. VAT is defined by variables for the percentage rate and for the proportion of purchases taxable (allowing for average exempt supplies). Finally in Figure 9.4, *Prices* can be set up either as fixed values or as a cost mark-up coefficient. There is a mark-up switch (*M/u Sw*) to the left of the table, which can be set to tell the model which is which. As you can see, *Repairs* are sold at cost-plus.

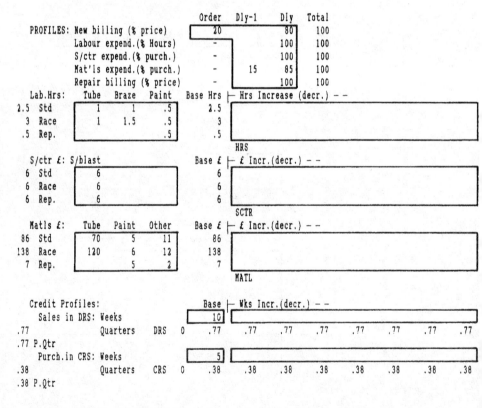

Figure 9.5 CYCLE1 Base Data: Profiles and Unit Cost Structures

Figure 9.5 shows some different types of data table. At the top are the *Expenditure* and *Sales billing* profiles, which are applied across all time periods. *New billings* for frames allows for a deposit to become due with order, in line with the order programmes that have been set up. Other billing percentages relate to sales programmes, and expenditure percentages relate to output programmes. The calculated totals ensure that those not adding to 100 can be seen and corrected.

Next in Figure 9.5 are three sections that define the cost structures of the three products. On the left, the *hours* and *pounds* can be entered in some detail and these base values are totalled across into the first quarterly column. The right-hand side of the tables allows for any projected savings or increases in cost to be entered across the other quarters. This is an economical way of entering data and is also a very effective way of allowing for 'what happens if?' type changes to be made later. It also shows very clearly where there are step changes in the data series. As before, these quarterly input tables are all named ranges and can be indexed by the current quarter reference number. On the left of Figure 9.5, the current quarter's data have been indexed. With these tables it will be the base values plus or minus the changes up to the current quarter.

At the bottom of Figure 9.5 are the *Credit Profiles*, which allow for entries to be made as base values, together with increases or decreases planned. They are set up as the number of weeks sales in debtors and the number of weeks purchases in creditors. These inputs are then recalculated into quarters for the model to handle. Again the current quarter is indexed on the left, but in this case the prior quarter is also indexed because both will be required in calculations from invoices.

Figure 9.6 shows the last part of the base data tables. At the top are variables related to direct workers. *Pay* is entered at a base level with changes allowed for in other quarters. This is converted to quarterly values as a named range for indexing. Also the *Number of workers* in each quarter can be entered, as averages for that quarter. In other words, if a new worker is to be taken on halfway through a quarter then the number in that quarter will include a half. This poor person, of course, has to suffer such an indignity so that we can calculate total pay in the quarter. Below this we need to enter total *Available Hours* in each quarter, so that total worker hours capacity can be related to total load hours to give overtime. There are two other variables required in this section, namely the *Overtime* rate, as a ratio to basic pay level, together with *National Insurance* as a percentage of pay, which is then extended as a coefficient.

The next section in Figure 9.6 allows for detailed overheads to be input, again as base values plus or minus changes in later quarters. There are, however, two lines in the change columns that are calculated and cannot be entered. The first is *Heat, light and power,* which calculates the change by taking the base value, dividing by the available hours for that quarter and multiplying by the overtime hours worked out by the prime cost module. This relates the electricity and heating costs to the time the factory is open. It could also have been seasonally adjusted, but this exercise simply shows the basic methods. The second calculated changes are for *Packing and delivery,* which are related to the increase or decrease in total sales quantities from base quarter to present quarter. A lot can be done to automate the calculation of overheads because so many of these costs can be defined by other parameters. The other changes that have been entered relate to planned acquisitions of new plant and vehicles.

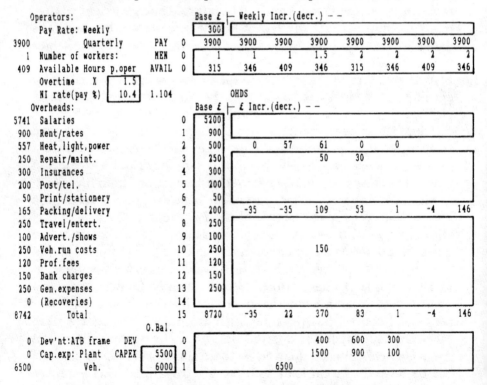

Figure 9.6   CYCLE1 Base Data: Operator Data, Overheads,
Development and Capital Expenditure

At the bottom of Figure 9.6 the *Development* and *Capital expenditure* figures can be entered, at base-quarter levels and in the quarter in which they are expected to be purchased. To the left of this table entries are also required of the opening balances of fixed assets, at cost. This is the end of the data input section proper although, as you will see as we work our way through the model, material purchase programmes have been squeezed in at the bottom of intermediate calculations and there are some more inputs dotted around the spreadsheet that are more logically located in other places.

Prime Cost Module

Before we look at the prime cost module proper, you will see at the top of Figure 9.7 the model heading and main switches. The key switch here is the *Qtr.Ref.* which determines which quarter is being run. When this is entered and the calculation command is given, then the model is run and shows the name of the quarter just to the right of the switch. This quarter name is repeated in all reports to ensure that all printouts can be properly identified. Also shown are switches, which escalate values and switch from calculating material purchases based on purchase programmes to purchases based on output programmes.

The *Prime cost module* calculates the *Cost of outputs* for the current quarter by indexing output programmes, unit costs and escalation factors, pushing part into the prior quarter according to the expenditure profiles. The *Materials purchased* in the quarter are also calculated and, if the material switch is set at zero, this will be the same value as purchases in outputs. *Sub-contract*, *Materials purchased* and *Labour hours* worked are then totalled for each quarter by overlaying each slice as quarters are calculated.

Below this the overtime hours are derived, so that total pay can be calculated from *Basic pay*, *Overtime* and *National Insurance* (company's contribution). The total pay bill divided by the hours worked then gives a cost rate per hour for each quarter, so that a complete cost of sales for the quarter can be calculated at the bottom. The total prime cost of sales is given a range name so that it can be indexed into the sales and profits module. The cost of *Warranty* repairs, which are of course not sold, are also calculated separately for the current quarter.

```
Short Term Forecast.      Qtr Ref. [    2]  1/94  Escal.Switch: [    1]  Mat.prog.Sw: [    1]
───────────────────────────────────────────────────────────────────────────────────────────
Prime cost module.     Prior Qtr.    1                              ** Materials
------------------                                                     Purchased:
Prime Cost of Outputs:        Labour Hrs:   S/ctr purch.£:  Matl purch.£:   Qtr:   1/94
    Qtr.      2       Ref  P.Qtr  C.Qtr   P.Qtr  C.Qtr   P.Qtr  C.Qtr   P.Qtr  C.Qtr
    Wty repairs            0      1       0     12      2     12       0      0
    Standard frame    0    0    350       0    846   1806  10311    1935  11047
    Racing frame      1    0     90       0    181    621   3545    1035   5909
    Repair/re-enamel  2    0     15       0    181     32    180     105    599
                         ------ ------  ------ ------ ------ ------  ------ ------
        Total            0    456       0   1220   2461  14048    3075  17555
              Sub-contract Purch. £                       Materials Purch. £
    Qtrs    2      3      4      5        Qtrs    2      3      4      5
     2    1220                             2   17555
     3     0    1595                       3    2993  17085
     4           0    1515                 4          3517  20081
     5                0    1211            5                2377  13574
     6                     0               6                       4235
    Totals 1220  1595   1515   1211       Totals 20548 20602  22458  17809
                                                       Labour Hours.
                                          Qtrs    1      2      3      4      5
                                           1     331
                                           2      0     456
                                           3            0     561
                                           4                  0     539
                                           5                        0     424
PAY £      1      2       3      4      5   6
  Basic  3900   3920    5909   7918   7958  Worked   331    456    561    539    424
  O/time    0    676     717      0      0  Avail.   346    409    519    630    692
  NI       406    478     689    823    828  O/time    0     47     42      0      0
  Total   4306   5074    7315   8741   8786
  P.Qtr  C.Qtr                          1      2      3      4      5      6
  .13.01  11.13  LRATE  Labour Rate £/Hr 13.01  11.13  13.04  16.22  20.72  20.82  20.9
Prime Cost of Sales:
   Qtr.     2     Ref  Mat'l   S/ctr  Labour         Total
   £                   purch.  purch.
                       ------  ------ ------         ------
   Standard frame  0   8655    604    2783          12042  PCOST
   Racing frame    1   4166    181    1002           5349        Warranty cost
   Repair/re-enamel 2   212    181     167            560        Qtr:    2
                       ------  ------ ------         ------               ------
                      13033    966   3952          17951                    37
                       ------  ------ ------         ------               ------
```

Figure 9.7 CYCLE1: Prime Cost Module and Headings

Sales and Profits Module

This module, in Figure 9.8, brings together the sales and costs of each product to show the contribution they each make to overheads and profit. The statement then goes on to offset the cost of overheads, any interest on loan capital and the cost of developing new products, in this case the mountain bike frame.

```
Sales & Profits:   for Qtr.   1/94
---------------                    Prime cost:  Gross margin:   Wty prov'ns:
                  Qty. Sw.  Sales  Ref                % sales   % sv              Profit
                  ---- ---  ------  ---  ------  ------  ------  ---  ------       ------
Standard frames    100  1   19500   0   12042    7458    38.2   .5     98          7360
Racing frames       30  1    8850   1    5349    3501    39.6  1.5    133          3368
                            ------       ------  ------                 ------     ------
     New sales              28350       17391   10959    38.7          231        10728
Repair/re-enamel    30  1     935   2     560     375    40.1            0          375
                            ------       ------  ------                 ------     ------
   All products            29285       17951   11334    38.7          231        11103
                            ------       ------  ------                 ------

Deduct:
  Overheads:
    Salaries                                                     5770
    Rent/rates                                                    907
    Heat,light,power                                              561
    Repair/maint.                                                 252
    Insurances                                                    302
    Post/tel.                                                     202
    Print/stationery                                               50
    Packing/delivery                                              166
    Travel/entert.                                                252
    Advert./shows                                                 101
    Veh.run costs                                                 252
    Prof.fees                                                     121
    Bank charges                                                  151
    Gen.exp.less recov.                                           252
    Depreciation                                                  752
      Total                                                     ------   10091
                                                                         ------
                                     Operating Profit                    1012
                                                                         ------
Interest on Bank borrowings                                                22
Development of mountain bike frame                                          0
                                                                         ------
                                     Net Profit, before tax               990
                                                                         ------
```

Figure 9.8   CYCLE1: Sales and Profits

The products can be switched in or out, so that the effect of a different product mix could be quickly evaluated. The prime cost of each product can be indexed by entering the reference number (0–2) alongside the *Prime cost* column. This facility is not really of any use in this particular model, but in a real business model the sales would probably be analysed by product within market or customer, rather than product only. There would then be a real need to pick up the cost on each line by indexing PCOST from the prime cost module in this way.

Also shown in this statement is a *Provision for warranty* against each product. This is calculated as a percentage of sales value, which would be set at a level sufficient to cover the average incidence of warranty repair cost predicted for each product, based on past experience. Warranty repairs, done free of charge, in this quarter will be charged against the provision balance built up out of sales in prior quarters.

Intermediate calculations

Figures 9.9 and 9.10 show the intermediate calculations of transactions and balances, that are needed for balance sheets and other statements. In addition, Figure 9.10 has a data table for *Material purchase volumes* at the bottom.

Figure 9.9 shows the straight line *Depreciation* calculations. The costs of *Additions* have been escalated to the quarter in which they are purchased and the asset lives have been set at 8 years (32 qtrs) for plant and 4 years (16 qtrs) for the new van. Acquisition is assumed to be mid-quarter, hence the first depreciation charge is for half the full quarterly charge.

Figure 9.10 has mostly calculations that are built up quarter by quarter, as the model is run. At the top, *Sales* come from the sales and profits module, but the value of orders has had to be constructed separately, using the order programme quantities. *Order value* is needed to calculate *Deposits* taken with orders. Other deposits and *Progress payment (PP) billings*, as well as *Sales delivery billings*, are calculated from sales, using the billing profiles. *Deposit liquidations* are needed to derive the balance sheet liability for outstanding customer deposits. They are calculated as the product of the total *Deposit and PP* percentage and the total sales in the quarter, for each product. Deposits will be liquidated, or offset against sales value, at the point of sale or delivery, so that only the balance of the sales price will be due.

Depreciation calculation:					0	1	2	3	4	5	6	7
		£	Qtrs o/s									
Open.bal: plant		4125	24		172	172	172	172	172	172	172	172
veh.		1500	4		375	375	375	375	0	0	0	0
Additions:		£	Qtrs Qtly Dep.									
Plant	0	0	32	0	0	0	0	0	0	0	0	0
	1	0		0		0	0	0	0	0	0	0
	2	0		0			0	0	0	0	0	0
	3	1523		48				24	48	48	48	48
	4	920		29					15	29	29	29
	5	103		3						2	3	3
Veh.	0	0	16	0	0	0	0	0	0	0	0	0
	1	0		0		0	0	0	0	0	0	0
	2	6549		409			205	409	409	409	409	409
	3	0		0				0	0	0	0	0
	4	0		0					0	0	0	0
	5	0		0						0	0	0
752	Total Depreciation:		DEPN		547	547	752	980	644	660	661	661

Figure 9.9 CYCLE1 Intermediate Calculations: Depreciation

The slices building up *Direct purchase invoices* are the prior and current year totals of materials and sub-contract purchases from the prime cost module. In the build up of *Other purchase invoices* below, overheads and development come from each quarterly run of the sales and profit statement. Capital expenditure (*Capex*) is the sum of plant and vehicle cost additions from the depreciation section (Figure 9.9).

VAT output tax is the sales total each quarter at the VAT rate. *Input tax* is the total of direct plus other purchase invoices multiplied by the percentage of purchases taxable and the VAT rate. The net VAT amount each quarter forms the balance due to Customs & Excise in that quarter. This is assumed to be paid in the following quarter. Interest is calculated on the average bank borrowings shown on the balance sheet, which we will look at next. The quarterly borrowing rate payable is entered and the equivalent annual rate is calculated below as a yardstick.

Other transactions & balance calc'ns:

| | Sales: | | Orders @ Sell.Value: | | -- | Sales & PP Billings £ | | | | | Dep.& PP |
Qtrs	New	Rep.	Std.	Race	Total	1	2	3	4	5	billings
1	25400	1303	29250	7800	37050	21623					7410
2	28350	935	39000	13650	52650	0	23615				10530
3	52800	1972	29250	11700	40950		0	44212			8190
4	44050	1979	23400	11700	35100			0	37219		7020
5	34250	1802	30000	15000	45000				0	29202	9000
6	37050	1414	30000	20000	50000					0	10000
Totals				Sales billings		21623	23615	44212	37219	29202	
				Dep.& PP billings		7410	10530	8190	7020	9000	
				Dep/PP liquidations		5080	5670	10560	8810	6850	

Qtrs	Direct Purchase Invoices £.	1	2	3	4	5
1		8282				
2		3075	18775			
3			2993	18680		
4				3517	21596	
5					2377	14785
6						4235
Totals		11357	21768	22197	23973	19020

| | Other Purchase Invoices £. | | | | | | | |
Qtrs	O/hds	Capex	Dev.	1	2	3	4	5
1	3485	0	0	3485				
2	3569	6549	0		10118			
3	3951	1523	404			5878		
4	3685	920	609				5214	
5	3630	103	306					4039
6	3652	0	0						3652
Totals				3485	10118	5878	5214	4039

VAT:	Output tax	4673	5125	9585	8055	6309
	Input tax	2208	4743	4176	4342	3430

IRATE

Interest on Bank borrowings:	Rate p.Qtr.	3.5		22	175	361	304	145
	- equiv.rate p.a.	14.75						

150	Mat'l purch.prog. :	Standard 0	100	100	150	150	100	100	150	150
50	[MATIN]	Racing 1	50		50	50	100	50	100	
100		Repair 2	100		100		100		100	

Figure 9.10 CYCLE1 Intermediate Calculations: Other
Transactions and Balances

Balance Sheets

The balance sheets, shown in Figure 9.11, are calculated in the
following way:

☐ *Stocks*: Each qtr: Bal.prev.qtr + inputs - outputs
☐ *Deposits*: All qtrs: Bal.prev.qtr - receipts + liquidations

- *Debtors* (DRS): Each qtr: Curr.qtr DRS profile × sales billings and VAT
- *Suppliers*: Each qtr: Curr.qtr CRS (creditors) profile × total purch.invoices and VAT
- *VAT balance*: All qtrs: Input tax - output tax
- *Fixed Assets @ cost*: All qtrs: Bal.prev.qtr + additions
- *Fixed Assets depreciation*: All qtrs: Open.bal. - cum.depr'n to date
- *Warranty*: Each qtr: Bal.prev.qtr - provisions + cost
- *Capital*: All qtrs: Open.bal. + cum.extra investment to date
- *Retained Profit*: All qtrs: Open.bal. + cum.profit less drawings to date
- *Bank balance*: All qtrs: Capital employed - (capital + retained profit)

Other figures, shown below on Figure 9.11, are:

- *Profit*: Each qtr: Net profit from Sales and Profit Module
- *Net Cashflow*: All qtrs: Prev.qtr CE + curr.qtr profit - curr.qtr CE

Again, as in previous diagrams, the boxes indicate the data entry areas. On the right you will see an *Average capital employed* calculation, which is used later to compare 'what happens if?' profit performances. You will also see two totals below, namely *Profit* and *Cashflow* for the year, which are used as check totals for the analyses of profit and cashflow at the bottom of the model.

Cashflow analysis

The cashflow analysis, in Figure 9.12, is derived as follows:

- *Customer receipts*: Bal.change + billings and VAT
- *PP receipts*: Each qtr: ((100-curr.qtr profile) +prior qtr profile) of PP bills

Payments to:

- *Suppliers*: Bal.change + purch.bills and VAT
- *Pay and benefits*: Each qtr: Salaries + wages (incl.employer's NI)
- *VAT*: Prev.qtr balance
- *Interest*: Part of intermediate calculations

Capital increases and drawings are both data input areas.

```
Balance Sheet:            1          2      3      4      5
--------------        Open.Bal.  Qtr.  1/94   2/94   3/94   4/94
                       -------         ------ ------ ------ ------
Stocks & WIP:  Finished    1600         6416   1380   1381   1380
               Lab. WIP     500          500    500    500    500
               S/ctract     100          100    100    100    100
               Mat'ls      2000         6039   5598   7238   8765
               P.Paymts
                          ------        ------ ------ ------ ------
               Gross       4200        13055   7578   9219  10745
        Customer deposits  -500        -2958  -2390  -1501  -2126
                          ------        ------ ------ ------ ------
               Net         3700        10097   5188   7718   8619

Customer Debts           24000        22130  41424  34861  27343

Suppliers               -10500       -13919 -12255 -12741 -10066
C & E for VAT            -2200         -382  -5409  -3713  -2879
                          ------        ------ ------ ------ ------
       Net current assets 15000        17926  28948  26125  23017
Fixed assets:
       @ Cost            11500        18049  19572  20492  20595
       Agg.Deprec'n      -6969        -7721  -8701  -9345 -10005

Warranty Fund            -300         -494   -897  -1282  -1567    Average
                          ------        ------ ------ ------ ------
       Capital Employed  19231        27760  38922  35990  32040    30789
                          ------        ------ ------ ------ ------

Financed by:
       Capital           15000        15000  15000  15000  15000
       Bank borrowings(bal) 1231       8770  11860   5486   2805
       Retained profit    3000         3990  12062  15504  14235
                          ------        ------ ------ ------ ------
                         19231        27760  38922  35990  32040
                          ------        ------ ------ ------ ------   Totals

Net Profits                            990   8072   3442  -1269    11235
Net Cashflows                        -7539  -3090   6374   2681    -1574
                                      ------ ------ ------ ------   ------
```

Figure 9.11   CYCLE1: Balance Sheets

```
CASHFLOW ANALYSIS:                     2       3       4       5      Total
    Receipts:  from Cust. Debts     30610   34503   51837   43029    159979
               deposits & PP's       8128    9992    7921    7475     33516
                         Total      38738   44495   59758   50504    193495
                                   ------  ------  ------  ------    ------
    Payments:  to Suppliers         33210   33915   33043   29164    129332
               Pay & benefits       10844   13113   14569   14643     53169
               C & E for VAT         2200     382    5409    3713     11704
               Bank for interest       22     175     361     304       862
                         Total      46276   47585   53382   47824    195067
                                   ------  ------  ------  ------    ------
    Trading cashflow                -7538   -3090    6376    2680     -1572
                                                                          0
    Increased capital                   0       0       0       0         0
    Drawings                            0       0       0       0         0
                                   ------  ------  ------  ------    ------
    Net Cashflow IN(OUT)            -7538   -3090    6376    2680     -1572
                                   ------  ------  ------  ------    ------
```

Figure 9.12   CYCLE1: Cashflow Analysis

```
SUBJECTIVE PROFIT ACCOUNT:             2       3       4       5      Total
    Sales                           29285   54772   46029   36052    166138
                                   ------  ------  ------  ------    ------
    Expenditure:Purchases - materials 20548  20602   22458   17809    81417
                         sub-contract  1220   1595    1515    1211     5541
                         overheads     3569   3951    3685    3630    14835
                         development      0    404     609     306     1319
            Pay & ben.- direct         5074   7315    8741    8786    29916
                         salaries      5770   5798    5828    5857    23253
            Depreciation charge        752    980     644     660     3036
                                   ------  ------  ------  ------    ------
                                   36933   40645   43480   38259    159317
    Stocks & WIP: opening            4200   13055    7578    9219     4200
             less: closing         -13055   -7578   -9219  -10745   -10745
    Warranty: provisions in sales     231     442     427     319     1419
             less: expenditure        -37     -39     -42     -34     -152
    Bank interest                      22     175     361     304       862
                                   ------  ------  ------  ------    ------
                                   28294   46700   42585   37322    154901
                                   ------  ------  ------  ------    ------
    Net Profit, before tax            991    8072    3444   -1270     11237
                                   ------  ------  ------  ------    ------
```

Figure 9.13   CYCLE1: Subjective Profit Account

Profit accounts

Both the *Subjective profit account,* in Figure 9.13, and the *Objective profit account,* in Figure 9.14, have lines that are picked up from other calculated transactions. Three of them are indexed from the sales and profit module each quarter, namely *Warranty provisions, Warranty expenditure* and *Prime cost.*

OBJECTIVE PROFIT ACCOUNT:	2	3	4	5	Total
Sales	29285	54772	46029	36052	166138
Prime cost	17951	34950	31033	26245	110179
	------	------	------	------	------
Gross margin:	11334	19822	14996	9807	55959
% of sales	38.7	36.2	32.6	27.2	33.7
Warranty provisions	231	442	427	319	1419
	------	------	------	------	------
Product contributions	11103	19380	14569	9488	54540
% of sales	37.9	35.4	31.7	26.3	32.8
Deduct:					
Salaries	5770	5798	5828	5857	23253
Overhead expenses	3569	3951	3685	3630	14835
Depreciation	752	980	644	660	3036
Interest on Bank borrowings	22	175	361	304	862
Development of mountain bike frame	0	404	609	306	1319
	------	------	------	------	------
Net Profit, before tax	990	8072	3442	-1269	11235
	------	------	------	------	------

Figure 9.14   CYCLE1: Objective Profit Account

Analysis of the forecast

The balance sheet, cashflow and profit reports of the model are showing a forecast, which is the result of running the model through from Qtr.1 to Qtr.7 with the data that has been input. What I will do now is to look at the prospects of the business, shown by this forecast, to see if there are any changes that could be made to improve performance. The model will then be run with these options to see, in each case, what the likely outcome would be.

Looking at the balance sheet, there would appear to be trouble brewing very fast in the bank borrowings department. There is a forecast jump in borrowings of £7,500 in Q1/94 and a further £3,000 in Q2/94, pushing the overdraft up to nearly £12,000 by mid-year. Assuming the bank facility limit is only about £1,500 at present, then something quite drastic will need to be done quickly. The bank, I suggest, would be unlikely to agree to such a large increase, even if the quarterly profits were forecast to rise rather than tail off. The owner of the business, I will also assume, would be unable to find another £10,500 to put in. The first course of action, therefore, must be to find a way rapidly to increase receipts or reduce payments, particularly over the first half of the year. If this cannot be done then, far from continuing to expand and to develop the new frame, the business would have to contract to a point where it might not survive.

The way that profits are tailing off also needs attention, though we could regard it as a secondary consideration at the moment. The root cause of this problem is the way that prices of new frames are held at present levels throughout 1994 and are only predicted to increase, by 2.5 per cent for the standard frame and 5 per cent for the racing frame, from the start of 1995. It may not be possible to bring increases forward without loss of business, so costs will need to be critically examined to see if savings can be made.

Other pointers to our cashflow problem can be seen from the balance sheet. Customer debts are very large. They represent ten weeks' worth of sales, whereas the business is having to pay suppliers within five weeks. Material stocks have increased considerably as well, which is no doubt a function of the buying policy. Quite a large amount of money gets locked up in this stock. In the first quarter this is compounded by a large stock of finished frames as well. Between them, these two stock increases cover the total overdraft in the first quarter. The size of material purchases, compared with total expenditure, can be seen from the subjective profit account. Cost savings in this area could be significant, even if the percentage change was comparatively small.

Possible improvements

Concentrating on the cashflow crisis, there are several courses of action that could be beneficial. First we should make some attempt to reduce the time it takes to collect the customer debts. Customers who will not pay up, particularly large customers, are often the bane of small businesses. There is always the fear that pressure to pay might mean loss of further orders. In this instance, though, most customers will not be that large and a two-week reduction in debt should be more than possible, starting straight away. The impetus for this action must be that there would be a permanent step change in the bank balance.

The investment in the new vehicle could be deferred for two quarters, which should move £6,500 in payments from the first to the second half of the year, as well as saving some running costs. There might not be any need to hire extra delivery capacity, since the sales increase takes place nearer to mid-year. However, extra running costs already allowed for could be left in from Q3/94.

The other investment, in materials, could also be reduced if the buying programme were to be brought into line with production needs, and materials were received immediately prior to building. The model has allowed for this to be easily changed by having a switch at the top. It might not be possible to change buying in this way. For example, the supplier might insist on certain minimum batch quantities. But perhaps there is an alternative supplier.

An extra worker has been forecast from halfway through Q2/94 to cope with the rising workload. It might be possible to spread back the output programme so that, with extra overtime, one direct worker could handle it. The extended working day would push up the cost of running the factory and a policy of dependence on overtime might put output at risk. We need to see what outcome in financial terms the model predicts. We could also see if a part-time worker, instead of full-time, could be taken on from Q2/94. Both of these options are not going to affect the first quarter of the year so they will not do much to reduce the overdraft. They may be worth doing though to bring down costs and push up profits.

Customer deposits could be a source of extra cash in the early part of the year, if the deposit required on all new orders was increased. It would not have an immediate effect with the current delay in customer payment. The percentage currently asked for is 20 per cent of price. It should be possible to increase this to 25 per cent, particularly as several competitors already quote these terms.

'What happens if?'

The results of running the model to test these changes are shown in Figure 9.15. The options presented are mutually exclusive and shown in comparison with the present forecast. The presentation shows *Profits*, measured against both *Sales* and *Capital employed*, as well as *Net cashflows*, measured by calculation of the NPV at a target discount rate of 15 per cent per annum. This discount rate assumes that the business wants to achieve this rate of return on its investment. A positive NPV will therefore show by how much the value of the business will increase after giving this return. At the bottom of the table is the *Maximum level of overdraft* required and the quarter in which that is expected.

Cycle Business : Forecast for Qtrs 1-4,1994.

£. escalated	Present forecast	A: Debtors @ 8 wks	B: New veh. deferred 2 Qtrs	C: Mat'ls just in time	D: Output spread: 1 worker + o/time	E: Add part time worker 94/Q2-4	F: Cust. deposits up to 25%
Sales total	166138	166138	166138	166138	166138	166138	166138
Net Profits total	11235	11815	12472	11511	11627	13874	11420
Average Capital Employed	30789	25736	28691	27804	30873	30742	29213
Profits: % to sales	6.8	7.1	7.5	6.9	7.0	8.4	6.9
% to ave CE	36.5	45.9	43.5	41.4	37.7	45.1	39.1
Net Cashflow: 1994/Q1	(7539)	(2760)	(2947)	(5143)	(8636)	(7539)	(5834)
Q2	(3090)	402	(1046)	(2370)	(4399)	(3090)	(2260)
Q3	6374	5147	1843	8002	7167	7092	5889
Q4	2681	1781	906	4491	5329	4753	2540
Total	(1574)	4570	(1244)	4980	(539)	1216	335
NPV of cashflow @ 15% pa.	(2166)	4031	(1423)	4073	(1400)	369	(238)
Max.cum.Bank borrowing	11860	3991	5224	8744	14256	11860	9325
- in 1994,Qtr	2	1	2	2	2	2	2

Figure 9.15   CYCLE1: Model Run Results

Option *A* is quite dramatic and demonstrates just what a two-week reduction in debtors can do for cashflow. The bill to the customer is, after all, the biggest figure in the product cashflow cycle. Having it paid is the key to getting back all your costs, profit and VAT. A modest 20 per cent improvement in this cash collection process changes the fortunes of the business immediately. If the payment delay was reduced still further to six weeks by the second quarter, the NPV would be over £11,000 and there would be a healthy £10,600 in the bank at the end of the year.

Deferring the purchase of a new vehicle in option B brings the overdraft down by an amount just greater than the vehicle cost. The effect on NPV though is distorted by the way supplier payments are averaged in the model. This purchase would in fact be paid for at a single point in time, but the credit profile will push $5/13$ths of it (plus the VAT) into the next quarter. The business model ought to handle these large purchases separately.

Purchasing materials just in time for production (option C) also has an impressive effect on NPV, but does not reduce the overdraft by as much. This is because the elimination of purchases for stock is spread over the year, rather than falling into the early quarters where funds are so scarce.

Option D allows for some of the workload to be done a bit sooner so that the programme is smoothed out, thus allowing a single operator to handle it, but it does not do much for bank borrowing. Although material stocks are reduced in the early quarters, the finished stocks significantly increase, giving a net stock increase. Payroll savings in later quarters contribute to an overall NPV improvement, however, which would be consolidated in the following year. The overtime level though, which peaks at about 16 hours per week in Q2/94, would be unlikely to be acceptable either to the hard-pressed worker or the manager, both of whom would worry about maintaining such an effort.

Option E shows the effect of taking on a part-time worker in Q2/94 for the rest of the year, rather than a full-time one. Although the overdraft remains the same, the NPV is again improved by reduced payroll costs in the last half of the year. This, perhaps surprisingly, is a better option than D, where the workload was spread and covered by overtime.

Option F gives sufficiently more cash up front to reduce the bank overdraft and it improves the NPV by about the same amount. As with the debtor reduction, it improves cashflow in early quarters, at the expense of later quarters, which is the sort of effect we were looking for. Once again it is clear how effective such a small change in terms of business can be.

Conclusions

Clearly the problems that the business is faced with can be dealt with completely by a combination of actions from the options that we have just looked at. Combined effects can, in some of these cases, be derived simply by adding together individual changes from the present case. The result of combining case *A* and case *F*, though, cannot be deduced in this way and needs to be run on the model because these changes are interactive. In any case, it is always quicker and safer to run the model again.

What this demonstrates, of course, is just how easily different courses of action can be devised by building and using a model in this way and how difficult it would be any other way. Once the model has been built, it becomes a very powerful tool, which can be used to look forward, see danger signs and decide upon actions that will keep the business operating successfully.

PART C: THE INVESTMENT DECISION MODEL CYCLE2

Model structure

Figure 9.16 shows the complete spreadsheet for the model CYCLE2, which has been built to evaluate a specific investment decision, namely whether or not to do shotblasting in-house or to continue to use a sub-contractor. The top part of the spreadsheet is the model proper, in the form of a report. Below is the data section. All input areas are shown within boxes.

Both the payments made to the sub-contractor, at *A*, and the payments made to do the job in-house, at *B*, have been evaluated. They have then been compared by deducting *B* from *A* to give *C*, which is the net cash saving as a result of doing it in-house. Both the NPV and DCF (discounted cash flow, or internal) rate of return are then calculated to measure the value of those savings.

The sub-contractor charges higher prices for smaller batch sizes, so programme quantities are analysed between these price levels in the data section. The in-house programme quantities will be the same as those bought out. In addition, there is an assumption made that the new plant could also be used to do work for other external customers. These *External sales quantities* are input down below.

Sub-contract v. In-house Shotblasting.   Escal.Switch: [1]   [Case 1.]

```
CASH PAYMENTS:           Year 1      2        3        4        5         Total
-------------            ------   ------   ------   ------   ------       ------

A. Sub-contract:
   -------------

   Purchases              8550     9776    11816    13386    14799        58327
                         ------   ------   ------   ------   ------       ------

   NPV @    [ 15 ]% p.a.                   25985    34787    43248


B. In-house:
   ---------

   Purchase shotblaster  [3500]                                           3500
   Installation costs    [ 400]                                            400
   Oper.costs: Labour     6500     6728     6963     7552     9316        37059
               Materials   225      273      352      436      512         1798
               Overheads  1740     2000     2575     3193     3750        13258
   Ext.sales:  Sw.  [ 1 ]    0     -286     -595    -1237    -1930        -4048
                         ------   ------   ------   ------   ------       ------
                         12365     8715     9295     9944    11648        51967
                         ------   ------   ------   ------   ------       ------

   NPV @    15 % p.a.                      26972    33510    40170


C. In-house NET CASH SAVING  -3815   1061     2521     3442     3151       6360
   ------------------------                                               ------

            - cumulative  -3815    -2754     -233     3209     6360
   NPV @      15 % p.a.                      -987     1277     3078
   DCF Rate of Return % pa.                   -3.6    30.9     44.3
```

```
Escalation coeff.: S/ctract  [ 1    1.04    1.0816   1.1249   1.1699 ]
                   Labour     [ 1    1.035   1.0712   1.1087   1.1475 ]
                   Mat/ohds   [ 1    1.04    1.0816   1.1249   1.1699 ]
Sub-contract:              Output quantities:
------------              Cost each Year 1     2        3        4        5
Batch size                incl.dely ------   ------   ------   ------   ------
[ 1 - 5      £     9.5 ]            900      950     1000     1000     1000
  6 - 10           7.5              50      150      200      300
  11 - 50            6                       50      150      150
                                   ------   ------   ------   ------   ------
                                    900     1000     1200     1350     1450

IN-house:          Time:
--------       MINS  HOURS   Qtys:
[ 1st 50   ]  [ 30 ] [ .5 ]  [ 50   ]
  Next 100     25    .417      100
  Rest         20    .333      750     1050     1300     1550     1750
                                      ------   ------   ------   ------   ------
                                       900     1050     1300     1550     1750
Total Hours worked                     316      350      433      516      583
O/time Hrs: basic  [ 500 ]    0        0        0        16       83  -- Overtime=Pay x  [ 1.5 ]
Labour pay pa.  £  [6500 ]                                            -- Pay & hours assume
Materials: £/100   [  25 ]                                              part time worker
Elec./Maint.: £/Hr [ 5.5 ]                                             becomes full time.
Ext.Sales: Qtys           [  0       50      100      200      300 ]   (extra 2 days)
           Price.£ [ 5.5 ]
```

Figure 9.16   CYCLE2: Investment Decision Model

In-house work is assumed to have a learning curve so that, in the first year, some jobs are assigned more time. The line of *Quantities* against the *20 min.* time does not have to be input, but is calculated as the total of sub-contracted plus external sales, less those input against the *30* or *25 min.* levels.

The total *In-house hours* worked are calculated from the quantities and job times and, below this, the hours that would have to be paid as *Overtime* are also shown. At the bottom left the value of *Materials* consumed is entered, at an estimated cost per 100 frames, as well as the incremental cost of *Electricity and maintenance* in running the plant, at a rate per hour. At the very bottom is the price at which *External sales* are expected to be made. This is set below the lowest price that is charged by the sub-contractor at present, on the assumption that this would be the only way to take part of his market.

The external sales have been provided with a switch in the model because we will want to see whether or not the case stands up without them. Switching them off cuts out the programme quantities in the model, so that both the sales and the costs get eliminated. These sales are really a spin off from being able to do the job. What we are looking at is the incremental effect of doing the job in-house. This applies also to the labour cost, where it has been assumed that an operator, presently working part time, becomes a full-time worker. The incremental labour cost of this operation is therefore the extra two days pay, plus overtime at time and a half.

The business case and possible flaws

On the face of it, the business case for in-house investment, shown by the model (*Case 1*) in Figure 9.16, is quite good. The business is forecast to achieve savings that give a target return by Year 4 and a rate of return of over 44 per cent per annum by the end of Year 5. The only problem seems to be whether or not the business could find an average of over £3,000 of extra capital for two years. Before going to the bank with this case we will need to understand what possible flaws there might be in it. If any contingencies could seriously damage the projected return we should take them into account in our decision.

The sort of things we will need to evaluate are, first, the case without external sales because we cannot be sure of getting this extra business. Second, we should understand the significance of the time it takes to do the task because, if these targets cannot be met, the extra costs of overtime or another worker could make the case untenable. Also, what happens if the operator gets sick or takes time off?

The sub-contractor might offer a price reduction if he thought we were going to enter the market for this work. Then, just how certain are the sales projections? The business might not be able to take the larger orders that allow it to take advantage of lower sub-contract prices for bigger batches. There may also be difficulties in installing the equipment, which cannot be seen at present, therefore the cost estimate may be low. So there are quite a few cases to be evaluated before we can be sure of our ground.

'What happens if?'

Figure 9.17 presents the results of these changes to the model. The different cases are described at the bottom and they are compared with our base case on the left. As with the previous model, I want to see the cashflows over the years, the time it takes to reach our target return (as measured by the NPV), the final return at Year 5 and the size and timing of the cash deficit, all as a result of doing the job in-house.

It appears that the following inferences can be drawn from these results:

☐ External sales, at the levels predicted, do not significantly influence the case.

☐ The case is very sensitive to the time taken to do the job. Only two minutes more per task destroys the case. So just how reliable is our estimate of timing?

☐ If the present sub-contractor really could be persuaded to drop his small batch price by £1, there would be little point in doing the job ourselves.

☐ Rather a lot depends on the operator, but there would not be too much damage done if he took up to two weeks extra time off in each year.

☐ Even if throughput remained about static and we would have paid top prices to the sub-contractor, it would still be worth doing the job in-house if we are prepared to wait a year longer for a much smaller return.

☐ The installation cost estimate would have to be wildly incorrect to make any real difference to the case, though any amount directly increases the need for front end capital.

Cycle Business.   Investment decision : Sub-contract v. In-house Shotblasting.

Evaluation of years 1-5. £. escalated	Base Case 1.	Case: 2.	3.	4.	5.	6.	7.
Net Cash Saving(Deficit) for in-house investment:							
Year 1	(3815)	(3815)	(4022)	(4715)	(3815)	(3815)	(4215)
2	1061	883	761	73	1061	779	1061
3	2521	2152	2134	1440	2198	1431	2521
4	3442	3018	1275	2317	1317	1908	3442
5	3151	3809	641	1981	666	2420	3151
Net Present Value @ 15%							
in Year 3	(987)	(1420)	(1747)	(3563)	(1231)	(2086)	(1387)
4	1277	564	(908)	(2039)	(364)	(801)	877
5	3078	2742	(542)	(907)	16	582	2678
DCF Rate of Return %							
in Year 5	44.3%	40.1%	7.9%	7.1%	15.2%	21.1%	38.7%
Cumulative Cash Deficit:							
Maximum level £	3815	3815	4022	4715	3815	3815	4215
- in Year	1	1	1	1	1	1	1
Cleared in Year	4	4	4	5	4	4	4

Changes made:
  Case 2. No external sales achieved.
  Case 3. In-house unit lab. time: only 22 mins achieved, not 20. (10% up)
  Case 4. Sub-contract unit cost: small batch price cut by £1 each, to £8.50. (10% down)
  Case 5. Operator: 2 weeks time lost each year (80 Hrs), so more overtime in later years.
  Case 6. Cycle frame outputs level off at 1000 pa. Larger orders (batches) not achieved.
  Case 7. Installation costs: problems cause estimate to double (to £800).

Figure 9.17   CYCLE2: Model Run Results

Conclusions

To decide whether or not to go ahead with this investment we would need more information, such as how far away the sub-contractor is, whether or not we have any choice of supplier, or whether production could flow better if we did the job in-house. The exercise has served to demonstrate how many factors can influence quite a simple business case. The case we have been evaluating does not look quite so encouraging now. Perhaps we should have tried to assess the probability of those problems occurring and used that to weight our NPV result. I think I will let you make the investment decision.

It is clear once again though, that the decision becomes that much easier and more rational when a model of the proposal is used to evaluate all the possible consequences. This is what I've tried to demonstrate in this chapter. I hope I have succeeded.

Index